I0198677

THE
CONSTITUTIONALIST
MANIFESTO
THE WOBBLING OF THE REPUBLIC

ANTHONY HORVATH

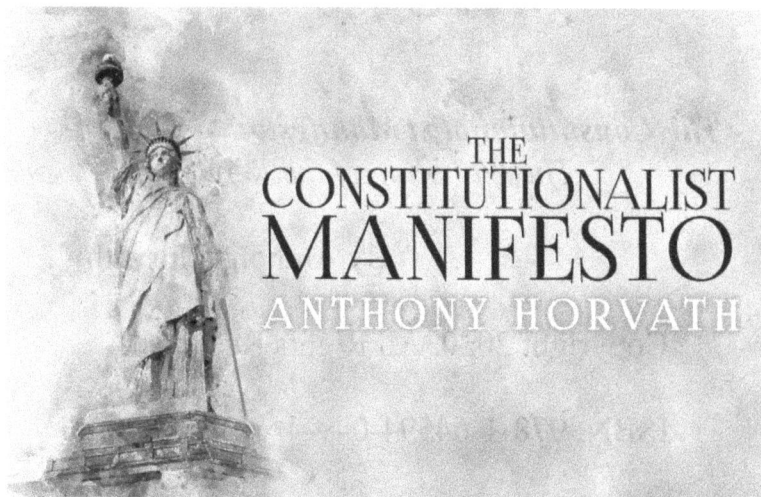

THE
CONSTITUTIONALIST
MANIFESTO
ANTHONY HORVATH

To Join the Conversation

Visit

www.constitutionalistmanifesto.com

The Constitutionalist Manifesto:
The Wobbling of the Republic

By Anthony Horvath

Copyright 2020, All Rights Reserved.

ISBN: 978-1-64594-049-4

When government fears the people, there is liberty. When the people fear the government, there is tyranny.

John Basil Barnhill

If only there were evil people somewhere insidiously committing evil deeds, and it were necessary only to separate them from the rest of us and destroy them. But the line dividing good and evil cuts through the heart of every human being. And who is willing to destroy a piece of his own heart?

Aleksandr Solzhenitsyn – *The Gulag Archipelago*

The work of human thought should withstand the test of brutal, naked reality. If it cannot, it is worthless. Probably only those things are worthwhile which can preserve their validity in the eyes of a man threatened with instant death.

Czeslaw Miłosz – *The Captive Mind*

Now there were some present at the same time who told him about the Galileans whose blood Pilate had mixed with their sacrifices. Jesus answered them, "Do you think that these Galileans were worse sinners than all the other Galileans, because they suffered such things? I tell you, no, but unless you repent, you will all perish in the same way. Or those eighteen on whom the tower in Siloam fell and killed them—do you think that they were worse offenders than all the men who dwell in Jerusalem? I tell you, no, but, unless you repent, you will all perish in the same way."

Jesus – Luke 13

Table of Contents

The Constitutionalist Manifesto

By Dr. Anthony Horvath
9/25/2020

Introduction

The last few decades have seen a fracturing of the United States which has seen voices on many and diverse sides warn of violence, and indeed, even civil war. When two of the largest states, California and Texas, each contemplate secession, but for exactly opposite reasons, you can be sure that something is seriously broken.

It may be said that the United States has always been a seething place. Except for a decade here or there, one may find throughout its history sustained periods of great tumult. Might it pull through now, as it always has?

Personally, I don't think so. Although I do not know what the shape and form will be of its final dissolution, nor the day of its fall, it seems to me that everything is conspiring to make it inevitable. I am not the only one to have come to this conclusion. However, having come to this conclusion, I have asked myself about what may come *after*.

There are many strong thinkers out there who see what I see and are striving to prevent such a great snapping. It is good that this is the case, because the United States is well worth saving and preserving. Beyond that, however, we must remember that if the United States failed, there would not only be a great cost to the country, make no mistake, there would be a great cost to the world, as well.

Those who love freedom, wherever they live in the world, arguably only have it right now because of our strong military. Our military draws strength from the integrity of our system. If our country descended into chaos, this would seep into our military as well. Tyrants who would expand their domains are currently deterred from doing so, but what if the people of the United States were forced to concern themselves only with internal affairs? Other oppressive regimes would gobble up territories around them, and worse. The collapse of the United States would be devastating to its own inhabitants, but would no doubt set the world on fire, as well.

Given this, should I then add my voice to these others? They have much larger audiences and intellects to match. My contributions in comparison would be meager. On the other hand, perhaps I could have an impact within my own, smaller, sphere of influence. The case can be made that I should throw my back into that effort, as well. However, the more I thought about it, the more I realized that while we have plenty of people engaged in the great project to preserve and repair the country, there are few, if any, men or women discussing what we ought to do *afterwards*, if all efforts are for naught. How should we rebuild if it comes to that?

No doubt, such a project is hindered right from the beginning because of such obvious factors as not knowing precisely how or when *after* has arrived.

Will each state go its own way? Will there be several splinter countries, rallying around California, Texas, New York, and Florida as nuclei? Perhaps it is worse than that, and even the various states fold. Maybe the larger cities will become 'city-states.' Will a thousand "CHAZes" spring up? Will there be war between the states? Or, will various regions re-align into new 'states'? Will other countries decide to take advantage of our weakness, even putting their own troops on the ground to seize *our* territory? Any particular scenario is unlikely but all are possible and impossible to predict.

Here, then, is what I propose to do.

I wish to initiate the conversation about how we should re-constitute *after* and facilitate the creation of organizations that would be ready to act at that time. At the same time, I wish to make these ideas 'backwards compatible.' That is, if the Union can be preserved, then we ought to preserve it, and I contend that the ideas I will present would indeed preserve the Union, if adopted (and actually implemented) in time.

That said, I doubt very much that these ideas will be adopted, for most of the principles undergirding them are already very well-known and could have been adopted in some form or fashion many times before now, but were not. Practically speaking, implementation will be *after*. Only then will people see the wisdom of the principles. Only then will the consequences for thumbing our noses at them be obvious enough to compel people to accede to them finally. Hindsight is 20/20, as they say.

Nonetheless, as a 'conservative' who considers the US Constitution to be one of the best political documents produced by mere mortals in all of human history, I think it is at least worth trying to make these ideas 'fit' into the existing Constitution, so that when it is all said and done, we can still say that the United States has continually existed since the late 1700's. It would be a shame, indeed, if we had to acknowledge that the United States of America is no more, and instead be left with poor shadows called 'The California Confederation' or 'The Republic of Texas.'[1]

Unfortunately, attempting to shoehorn these principles into the US Constitution requires modulating them at least a little. In some cases, the modulation is quite substantial. However, I deem it worth it. On the off chance that the Republic can be preserved by amending the existing Constitution and thus remaining within its framework, I will endeavor to accommodate the Constitution. With it being just as likely that the Republic will splinter or collapse, I will simultaneously present the principles more abstractly, so they can be brought to bear with much less baggage if we are forced to do a 'fresh start.'

Readers should remember throughout that my attempts to reconcile these principles with our existing system of governance reflect a 'last ditch' effort to save the Republic. In reality, it is those who read this

---

[1] No offense to Texans intended, but your forbearers affirmed long ago that despite how great Texas is, it is greater still when standing aside the other states of the Union.

after that are my main audience. I strongly suspect that people who are not all that receptive to my thoughts now will find them much more amenable after. And to the hasty dismissals of my proposals as 'impractical' because our system is thoroughly established, I state again that I am writing with the assumption that the system has thoroughly collapsed. Whether or not my proposals are impractical in that context is impossible to know at this point in time.

Progressives, socialists, and communists[2] will not find much that they like in this document. It is they that have played an outsized role in crashing the Constitution to begin with. In whatever calamity befalls our country, there seems little doubt in my mind that it will more or less pit the 'left' against the 'right,' but the outcome is not by any means assured. It should go without saying that if the 'left' prevails, the principles espoused in this document have as little chance of being implemented as a rainstorm occurring on the sun.[3]

I can only sense the outlines of the coming conflict but I do know that the cause of Freedom must win. It

---

[2] Notice I do not mention 'liberals.' The people we call liberals today are not liberals. They have appropriated a word that refers to something quite different than what it meant originally, compelling us to try to recapture that meaning in the phrase 'classical liberalism.' In other words, I am more of an actual liberal than they are! It would be nice to rescue the word from its abusers, therefore I do not use it to describe them. To be perfectly frank, your modern day 'liberal' is just another progressive at best, and proto-communist at worst.

[3] I further suspect that if things come to pass as I believe they will, many 'leftists' will look with horror upon their previous viewpoints and will be more interested in the ramblings of a constitutionalist. A man can dream.

must. Although I have much to say about them, the methods and machinations which secure that victory are outside the scope of this document. Yet I repeat: FREEDOM MUST WIN.

Big Government is the Problem

Big Government is the problem.

It doesn't matter who is in charge of it, whether they be noble or be scoundrel, Republican or Democrat, competent or incompetent. The bottom line is this: the bigger the government, the greater the incline towards tyranny or totalitarianism or both.

Because of the nature of Big Government, the scoundrels come to dominate, the party favoring the idea of Big Government comes to control it, and the incompetent come to fill the ranks. In order to understand why this is the case, we need to say a few words about the nature of government in general, so that we can understand what happens as it increases in size—as it always does.

In this era of willful illiteracy, I am forced to state that I am not against 'government', *per se*. Indeed, I am very much 'for' it. Hence the word 'big' in the phrase "Big Government." It is there for a reason! The truth is that there is no escaping some form or shape of government, so, insofar as it is within our power, our goal should be to establish the best government we can, and oppose that which the bad governments tend to achieve.

Understanding that even the best government will veer towards corrupt oppression is essential in laying the foundation for that good government. This is where the framers of the US Constitution shined. They understood that so many of their problems were the result of governance gone awry, so they built a system with checks and balances they thought would be adequate to the task. (They were wrong. These checks and balances were not sufficient, which is why I am writing this manifesto.)

In one of the *Federalist Papers*, James Madison laid out the challenge in this way:

> But what is government itself, but the greatest of all reflections on human nature? If men were angels, no government would be necessary. If angels were to govern men, neither external nor internal controls on government would be necessary. In framing a government which is to be administered by men over men, the great difficulty lies in this: you must first enable the government to control the governed; and in the next place oblige it to control itself.

In fact, men are not angels. Indeed, angels do not govern men. Unfortunately, the checks and balances they enacted were hamstrung from the beginning and have only limped along since. I will be delving into some of the reasons for that, but it is worth mentioning too that when Madison was thinking of the people[4] being the ultimate 'check' he was thinking

---

[4] He goes on immediately to say, "A dependence on the people is, no

of a particular population with its distinct culture. John Adams described this population thusly,

> Our Constitution was made only for a moral and religious People. It is wholly inadequate to the government of any other.

The framers certainly countenanced the possibility that the people may cease to be moral or religious, but they must not have thought it too likely, as the Constitution does not include the necessary mechanisms to preserve liberty if the people abandon first principles. The framers were counting on a population capable of *self-governance*. We no longer have such a population.

I invoke the term 'self-governance' deliberately. As I said above, you cannot escape some shape or form of government. This begins with the individual. If the individual is given to anarchy of the mind, the individual will still be governed, but by his instinct and, by definition, unbridled passions.

Likewise, properly understood, everyone is moral and religious, even the most devout atheist. What distinguishes people is what they choose to worship (for all worship something) and what the grounding for their morality is. When Adams and the other founders speak of "a moral and religious People" it is not, therefore, just any moral and religious people, but specifically people who are Christians. In short, with a

---

doubt, the primary control on the government; but experience has taught mankind the necessity of auxiliary precautions." This is an understatement, as it turns out.

population that is no longer predominantly Christian, but having a framework of governance presuming such a population, all bets are off, and have been for almost a century, if not longer.

This is not to disparage anyone who is not a Christian. However, if you happen to be such a person, and also someone who wonders why the country has gone crazy, you may wish to consider the possibility that this reality has something to do with it.

Just what that 'something' *is* is well beyond the scope of this document, and manifests in various ways over time, anyway. In our current time, however, the 'religious' spirit is shown in the astonishing politicization of literally everything. My contemporaries know that this is not hyperbole.

This is a recipe for disaster, as there is no meaningful sense in which the US Constitution is compatible with such omni-politicization. It should surprise no one that those engaged in omni-politicization detest the US Constitution and welcome Big Government with an enthusiastic embrace. They view checks and balances with hostility.

There are many people who have observed that the politicization of literally everything almost as an article of faith does not actually make adherents to this new 'religion' any happier. In fact, it makes them miserable. It makes the people around them miserable. It makes any society that is filled with such people miserable. Omni-politicization creates a perpetual state of rage, because what is at stake for them is not merely the perfection of society, but the very fulfillment of their reason for living, and *you* are standing in their way. *You* are preventing them from having a happy, satisfied, meaningful life. If only *you* would give into their demands... The problem being that the very nature of their itch is such that it can never be scratched, and demands will always follow demands, no matter how much you give into them.

Many have observed this, but it misses the really critical point. We are not just talking about unhappy and unhealthy people, or the collective misery that comes from the masses deriving purpose from politicizing everything. We must ask the question directly: "What does it mean to politicize something?"

It is not merely disagreeing about something, or disputing something, or arguing about something, or trying to sort out the truth about something. To say that something is *politicized* is to say that it is something that is subjected to the political process. It is something which is ultimately settled by a vote, and for these people, a 50.01% majority is more than enough to justify imposing the conclusion on the other 49.99%.[5] Is the matter something trivial, such as whether or not you can drink a 32 oz soft drink? No matter! Bring in the politicians, anyway!

Is it an imposition of the will of 150,000,000 on 149,999,999 people? Progress cannot be delayed even a single day on account of 'selfish' individuals who

---

[5] Unless, of course, they are in the 49.99%, in which case they plead for minority protections... while they muster up the resources to force another vote, and another, and another, and throw bricks through your windows, because "This is what democracy looks like!" Ya know?

do not agree with you, no matter how substantial the size of the lot of them. Naturally, you can be as angry as you like about such people, but more than that, you can do whatever you want to them, because, well, did we mention that they are selfish? They totally deserve losing their jobs, having their businesses burned down, being punched in the face, and so on, and so forth. Right? *Right?*

It will not do to say that it is no big deal because many of these issues and topics are relatively unimportant, so even if the 'democratic' imposition does occur, it should be something that everyone else should be willing to brush aside as inconsequential. Quite the opposite. If, perhaps, there were only one or two such impositions, it could indeed be brushed aside. After all, what is the alternative? Violent resistance because they won't let you buy a large soft drink? No one wants to resort to violence to object to impositions on trivial matters. But remember, this is the politicization of *everything*, and that is *not* hyperbole. So it is that such things occur repeatedly at a variety of levels of government.

This being the case, even if you find meaning and purpose in something quite apart from politics, you don't dare detach yourself from the political process. Who knows what could be done to you if you were not paying close enough attention? It is bad enough seeing what is being done to you while you are paying attention.

Whatever your view of God is, it is clear that you would have to actually be God in order to know the details of what is being enacted against you at any given moment by this or that agency, this or that legislator, judge, or executive.

Why, exactly, is it such a big deal that the most minute aspects of human existence are increasingly being managed via the political process? What is the problem with giving governments further and farther away from us more and more of our lives to manage?

People act as though it doesn't really matter if it is the government that does something as opposed to the individual, an organization, or a corporation, if the thing was 'good.' The argument is, "If it was right to do, who cares if it is a government that does it?"

To answer this question, we must take what will seem, at first, to be a detour.

The Nature of The Leviathan

I read once that the reason why the Republican Party has the elephant as its icon is because elephants have good memories, and Republicans are known to be animated by the lessons of the past. This makes them natural allies of the framers of the Constitution, who drew lessons from the history of the places they fled.[6]

Since that time, more history has unfolded. In the main, the framers were shown to be right about the

---

[6] We would do well to remember that the United States was initially founded by people trying to escape persecution at the hands of their own governments. We would also do well to remember that there is no longer any place one can go to escape persecution. If America falls, at present there is no place left to go.

things they worried about. The most obvious examples are in the 20th century, such as the tens of millions that died because of various fascist governments and the hundreds of millions that died because of the various communist governments. What they all had in common: governments. In the 20th century, far more people were killed by their own governments than were killed by foreign armies.

We should not forget this fact, and indeed, we should keep it front and center in our thinking. However, we also should not forget the history that the framers would have had in mind, either. Remember, they did not have the convenience of being able to look at numerous examples of successful republics. Back beyond the feuding royal families, there was also the tradition of resolving conflicts by murder and vigilantism.

Enter Hobbes[7] and his *Leviathan*.

The idea was simple enough. Remove the right to use violence from the citizens and vest it in a centralized authority that has enough power to overmatch anything that any individual citizen might be able to bring to bear. The citizens are satisfied with this because, in exchange, they do not have to worry that some other citizen with a grudge will bludgeon them over the head, because the begrudged citizen has to worry that Leviathan is going to exact justice upon them. The 'deal' only works, however, if Leviathan acts justly and with discretion.

The American Revolution was fought a little over a

---

[7] Lived 1588 to 1679.

century later, and one can gather from the writings of the revolutionaries that they perceived that history had revealed fairly well just how dangerous such a powerful government could be to the citizens. In fact, because of their *experience*, and the *experiences* of their own parents and grandparents, they feared powerful centralized authorities so much that they asserted in their Declaration of Independence these startling words:

> That whenever any Form of Government becomes destructive of these ends, it is the Right of the People to alter or to abolish it, and to institute new Government, laying its foundation on such principles and organizing its powers in such form, as to them shall seem most likely to effect their Safety and Happiness.

Then, they proceeded to put into their founding document the right of each individual to bear armaments so that if the government needed to be abolished, the people would have the tools necessary to do the job. So much for the Leviathan!

This intense distrust for centralized power notwithstanding, the founders were equally worried about vigilantism and mob violence. They recognized the value of having a system which discouraged wanton violence, because they no more wanted to be bludgeoned by a person with a grudge than anyone else did.

They attempted to strike the balance by establishing

a republic. In this republic, checks and balances would keep the government from getting out of control, but the citizens would not need to resort to violence to settle their conflicts. Instead, they could work out their differences legislatively. It was a good deal as far as deals go.

Now, this formula only works in the long term if certain conditions are in place, and to understand why, we have to think through everything we just said about the Leviathan's monopoly on violence.

Why is it different if the government does something compared to if an individual, organization, or corporation does it? Because according to the terms of the deal, only the government is allowed to bring violence to bear on those who don't go along with things, *that's* why.

It is astonishing how few people recognize the import of this so let us say it again to make sure it gets its due weight: on the terms of the deal, the people give up resolving conflict via violence and give the State a monopoly on the use of violence, leaving to the people the political process to work out their differences... which means that whatever the people decide via the political process, the State is able to implement... violently, if it deems it ultimately necessary.

If it was the case that something was unequivocally 'good,' then maybe, just maybe, it wouldn't be a problem if it was the government doing it, and not an individual, organization, or corporation. In the real world, however, very, very, very, very few things are deemed unequivocally 'good.'

Whatever proposition you wish to propose, there are going to be people who have some problem with it. If it is an individual, organization, or corporation doing the proposing, and an individual, organization, or corporation implementing the proposal, then the people who have a problem with it need not be involved. They don't have to associate with the individual, join the association, or buy the corporation's product. They can disagree, mildly or strongly, but at any rate, they don't have to participate. The displeasure is solely confined to their own brain.

Not so, if it is something the government is doing. If it is something the government is doing, then all of those being governed must participate, even if that participation means only being compelled to subsidize it via their taxes. A reason why we are where we are right now is because, naturally, people aren't only being forced to pay for things they don't agree with but they also must participate in it or comply with it.

Or don't comply, and go to jail, if you're lucky. If they come to arrest you for refusing to pay your taxes or comply with this or that ever-more intrusive law, and you resist, they can shoot you. Legally.

In sum, whatever the government becomes involved in inextricably becomes linked with and enmeshed in the government's power to compel compliance via, if necessary, violent coercion.

If it was just one or two things here and there over the centuries, the republic could survive.

Unfortunately, it has been one or two hundred thousand things, accumulating and compounding. It should not surprise anyone that many people are extremely unhappy with a large number of things that they are compelled to participate in and subsidize. And that's just the items from a time when theoretically things weren't thoroughly political. Imagine this present moment, when people are gleefully trying to politicize *everything*.

The Terms of the 'Deal,' Violated

I said above that the formula only works if certain conditions exist. Those conditions have not existed for a long time. Indeed, they began deteriorating even before the Constitution was ratified. It certainly did not help that the Declaration of Independence boldly claimed that all men were created equal even as the various states chose to tolerate a situation that allowed some men to be treated unequally, and in brutal fashion. As it happens, flatly contradicting the words actually written down and agreed to via the political process was a harbinger of things to come.

The first condition which made the formula of the US Constitution actually work was its carefully crafted, very small, list of things the Federal government was allowed to do. The underlying principle is simple, but has rarely been tried: the scope of what is actually permitted by the government to do must be very narrow, and confined only to those things which truly are matters which a large majority believe are properly the domain of the government. This must be the case, because there is such wide disagreement among all people on issue both great and small, to have all of these matters settled by the government... that is, have one group of individuals have their own particular opinion given the coercive power of the state... is a recipe for exactly what we are witnessing right now. The founders understood this, and they presumed this, and they built it right into the country's foundational document—only to have the principle ignored and disregarded almost before the ink was dry.

Are there topics which a majority believe are an appropriate place for the government to be involved? The founders had their own list, which, not coincidentally, they put in the Constitution. I would bet most wouldn't object *much* to the items in their list and would include it in their own.

For example, the founders handed the management of our currency over to the Federal government (Congress, in particular). Now, if the government could *only* regulate the currency used throughout the nation, and did very little else, there wouldn't be *much* to argue about for most people. If, on the other hand, the government can regulate what you are allowed to eat or drink, what kinds of vehicles you can use, where you can live, how you must build your homes, what kinds of trees you must or must not plant, what kind of nozzle you can have on your gas cans, when and where your children must go to school and what they must (and must not) learn, etc., etc., etc., etc., then for all practical purposes, the Deal is Dead.

The infinitely expanding scope and reach of the government—that is, the opinion of one (usually very small) group of people—into our lives makes it inevitable that there will be *many* examples where everyone else will believe that things have gone too far. Adding insult to the injury of being forced at gunpoint due to the State's monopoly on power, they also have to pay for it with their taxes.

One might say that if someone feels so strongly about it, they can muster up a campaign to have the law changed. Certainly, they could. And if it was just a handful of topics in the course of a life-time which have enraged them, that is precisely what we would commend to them, and precisely what the founders envisioned. But when it is ten thousand of them, there is no practical recourse. Only rage.

The second condition which makes the formula work is that when legislation actually is passed, it must actually matter. Remember, in America, the political process is a proxy for getting one's way via violence. Thus, instead of mustering up an armed gang or mounting a war among the various states, the differences are sorted out via legislation, which the people agree to abide by. They agree to abide by it because the alternative is to shoot people or be shot, so as long as the things settled via the legislature do not cut too close to the quick too many times (see the first condition), a civil society can be had.

Besides not being murdered in the street, the

legislative process holds out the hope that via persuasion of your countrymen, you could eventually attain a position where previous legislation that you didn't agree with was reversed or your own legislation was enacted. It is not uncommon to hear warm and fuzzy comments about how 'compromise' is the engine of peace in our country. Not exactly. What brings peace is the chance for the losers of elections or legislative battles to work hard and eventually have their own values prevail in the law.

Tragically, American history is chock full of examples where the people worked through their legislature, just as they were supposed to, only to have that legislation effectively nullified. Politicians may flaunt the legislation, courts might ignore it, or the wealthy and connected find a way around it. What tends to *actually* happen is that legislation is made to apply to people who do not have the time or financial resources to fight the law as written, while people with power and resources skirt the law with impunity. That is to say, the legislative process is *weaponized* against the people instead of being a vehicle for the people to govern themselves.

Examples of this are so numerous and varied that a retelling of them would take whole volumes. I'm sure readers can think of a few dozen almost immediately. Rather than get into particulars, let us consider the implications.

If the 'deal' is that we will resolve our differences via legislation, backed up by the coercive power of the state, but then that legislation is summarily dismissed, contorted, and corrupted, people begin to think they are the only ones playing by the rules. If this happens often enough on matters of increasing importance that are increasingly intrusive, you can easily see why people will eventually decide there is no point at all in playing the game.

Oh, they'll 'play' it, for a time. Not because they believe they have a fair shot in the political arena, but because they know that if they don't play it, the State can shoot them. 'Legally.' How long a society can last when such currents are swirling around, I don't know, but it can't be very long.

The role in the Supreme Court in corroding our system is especially pernicious, which I will discuss even more below. If the 'deal' requires us to substitute the legislative process for violence, then the legislation, as originally written and as originally understood, must be respected by all. But, if the Supreme Court can come in and completely ignore the text or even re-write it per their own whims, that whole idea where the legislative halls are the 'battlefields' which defuse the need for actual physical violence is completely short-circuited. Horrifically, the Supreme Court can and does do just this.

Compounding all of this is the fact that the people passing ever-intrusive laws show no indication of relenting. If anyone disagrees with either their mindset or their specific proposals, they blast them as 'selfish.' They insist that the 'selfish' people should not be so annoyed, because, after all, they worked through the 'system.' And by working through the 'system' they mean something absurdly dishonest like having the Supreme Court blatantly contradict words actually on the paper or pointing out that some nameless bureaucracy three miles deep and a thousand miles away considered your request before denying it. Naturally, with no appeal possible.

In such a climate, it is inevitable that 'well-meaning' souls will push and push and push and push until finally, at long last, the people just won't play the game anymore. What you do to them, you do by the threat of force. You just don't know it yet. One day you will.

This is the day that I believe is fast approaching because, for all practical purposes, the Deal is Dead.

The third condition is expressed by Thomas Paine, found in his pamphlet called *Common Sense*. In this pamphlet, he was laying out arguments for why America should be independent from England. This was just one of his arguments:

> As to government matters, it is not in the power of Britain to do this continent justice: The business of it will soon be too weighty, and intricate, to be managed with any tolerable degree of convenience, by a power, so distant from us, and so very ignorant of us; for if they cannot conquer us, they cannot govern us. To be always running three or four thousand miles with a tale or a petition, waiting four or five months for an answer,

which when obtained requires five or six more to explain it in, will in a few years be looked upon as folly and childishness— There was a time when it was proper, and there is a proper time for it to cease.

Paine was quite right: great distances and immense complexities make governing justly impractically difficult. We still have great distances and immense complexities. Just as it was "folly and childishness" to think that Britain could rule the American continent from three or four thousand miles away, it is "folly and childishness" to think that Washington DC can rule the American continent, which runs almost three thousand miles from sea to sea, and farther still if we include Alaska and Hawaii.

Let us distill this argument into a principle which we can apply in this present work. Essentially, in order for a civil society to remain civil, it must be practically possible for people to control how they are governed on the matters that are most important to them. The only way that this can be done, practically speaking, is to have the most intrusive measures imposed upon them by the level of government nearest to them. The further and farther away the level of government, the less impact on the individual's daily life that government should be allowed to have.

A corollary of the same is that a level of government should be permitted to consider only those measures which directly concern the specific population in question. If an issue concerns Town A but not Town B, C, or D, then the county that contains them all should be prohibited by design from being able to take action on the issue. If the issue concerns them all and rises to a level of seriousness that requires joint conciliation, then by all means, perhaps the county should address it.

As with towns and counties, so with counties and states. As with counties and states, so with states and the Federal government. If, that is, you want to maintain a civil society that does not eventually descend into violent clashes.

In the United States, the most vivid example of this principle being violated is the way that the Supreme Court is able to run roughshod over the democratically expressed wills of literally tens of millions of individuals. Here we see the convergence of a swirling storm of effects that come from dispensing with our first and second conditions.

On the one hand, the most intimate and 'trivial' matters along with the most important come before the Court to be decided. On the other hand, once these matters get to the Court, justices have been given leeway over the centuries to flatly ignore, disregard, and corrupt the various legislative texts, as written, and have even been permitted to invent language, policy, and even *de facto* legislation, out of nothing but their own minds.

Having been given such wide deference by Americans since *Marbury vs. Madison* (1803!) the Court has effectively become a quasi-oligarchy subverting what was designed to be a constitutional republic. People who think this is a great method for 'perfecting' society fail to understand that in the long term, they are shooting themselves in the foot. For, if the Court can behave this way, and does, what is to keep citizens from simply deciding that it is pointless to settle differences in our legislatures? Why bother? Won't people eventually adopt for their own personal policy the one attributed to President Andrew Jackson, "[Supreme Court Chief Justice] John Marshall has made his decision; now let him enforce it!" ? Or the still older policy: "*Molon Labe!*" ?

'Progressives' retort that this is 'no big deal' because using the courts in this way is still happening according to the parameters of the 'system.' However, remember that the 'system' was erected to turn down the heat in our public affairs by giving people a fighting chance for genuine self-government. This was accomplished by placing important deliberations within the reach of ordinary citizens. Now consider the difficulties of overturning a Court decision.

The most decisive way to deal with a Court decision should one desire to do so would be to pass a constitutional amendment which negates and contradicts the decision. The provisions for passing such an amendment, however, are purposefully difficult. It certainly should be difficult to alter the fundamental document governing the entire nation, but as a tool for dealing with innumerable offensive decisions, it is so unwieldy that we must confess the tool cannot be used at all.

The next obvious way is to change the people on the Court so that they are the kind to rule in your favor. However, with the doctrine of *stare decisis* in place, even a friendly Court justice will be disinclined. So, even here, there is little remedy for reversing the innumerable offending court decisions that are out there.

There are, of course, other ways, as well, of reining in the courts. The problem with all the methods is that they all basically require getting a veritable supermajority of hundreds of millions of people to go along with it, whether it be by having a sufficient number of states ratify the new amendment, or getting tens of millions of people to elect your desired person to the presidency, where, hopefully, he will appoint a satisfactory justice. Then, you need the senate to confirm the justice, and obviously you have no ability to cast a vote for any of the senators but your own, which means that this part is completely out of your control. Then you need a case that is similar to the one that set the precedent you so oppose to enter the system, which, by definition, will have to be some entity violating the 'law' to bring the matter to a head, which entails its own difficulties. Then, assuming that you've been able to do this at least *five* times, hopefully your justices will have the courage to rule in your favor.

Compounding this silliness is the fact that having SCOTUS rule in your favor probably means asking them to enforce their will by *fiat*, just as the initial offending case was also by *fiat*. In other words, whether 'for' or 'against,' whatever the matter was, it was probably not within the domain of the Court to act in the first place.

In short, this 'system' has just the same effect as the realities that Thomas Paine was complaining about as seen in the quote above. We would do well to remember that the first time around, the result was a bloody revolutionary war to resolve the problem. With such a 'system' as we now have as concerns the Supreme Court, no one should be surprised at all by the superheated rhetoric and worse that accompanies the appointment of a justice today. No one should be surprised if this, too, proves to be a catalyst for bloodletting, all the more when we remember the innumerable matters of huge importance decided by five individuals, rather than by the citizens themselves.[8]

This is the most vivid example, but it is not by any means the only one.[9] Some others are worth looking at

---

[8] Naturally, there are people who completely embrace the idea that the fate of 350,000,000 can and should be settled decisively by just five individuals (a 5-4 vote). These tend to be the same mouth-breathers who complain that the president is determined via electors rather than the popular vote. These same are ecstatic when 5 people overrule 60,000,000 provided the 5 justices are ruling in their favor. If they don't, there is weeping and gnashing of teeth about the decision and cries about the democratic process being thwarted. There is no pleasing such hypocrites, and if not for the fact that these people will probably be the first to shed blood in whatever is about to befall us, there would be no point in trying to engage them at all. They are beyond the reach of reason. However, as things escalate, I suspect that more and more people, even in this 'camp,' will begin to see the foolishness of this 'system.'

[9] The other obvious example is the President. If the President was restricted to doing only what was authorized by the Constitution, there would be much less reason to be so concerned about who was given the job. If, however, the President can do just about anything he wants, with access to a bureaucracy numbering more than a million people across hundreds, if not thousands, of agencies and departments, then the Presidency becomes

in order to fully understand the principle being discussed because as argued above, it isn't just the major issues that cause problems. The accumulation and compounding of issues big *and* small creates a suffocating atmosphere. Even though people can't quite put their finger on the reasons *why* they are having trouble breathing, they do know that their chests are constricting.

What does California have to do with Kentucky? Or Montana with Missouri? New Mexico with New York? There are very few issues that *reasonably* justify governmental actions that are shared by states so distantly separated.

Presuming, for the sake of argument, that California's policies on forest management are wise and judicious, it doesn't follow that their policies would make sense thousands of miles away. Indeed, people in Ohio may believe that California's policies, if applied to Ohio, would be devastating to the people of Ohio. Perhaps there is no great movement within California to impose its policies on forest management on the country, but there are plenty of other matters related to the environment that the politicians of California very much would like to impose on their countrymen outside of the state.

---

something so important that people believe it is worth fighting for. And by 'fighting' I mean resorting to violence. It is maintained by nearly all sides that thousands will die depending on who the president is, so what greater cause is fighting for the presidency? I said 'nearly all sides' because there is at least one position, *mine*, which evades the whole problem by insisting it is stupid to put the literal lives of so many into the hands of someone elected by some 65 million people or so.

None, it should go without saying, have any right to vote in California, which would make the rest of the country suffer from a variation of the maxim "no taxation without representation."

California politicians, activists, and bureaucrats are aware of their inability to directly shape the policies of other states, which is why they attempt whenever they can to empower the Federal government to do their bidding. Nonetheless, it remains a raw fact that there is little chance that what makes sense on the west coast will make sense elsewhere in the country.

The number of scandalous applications of 'one size fits all' impositions of Federal policy is grating to anyone who cherishes freedom, liberty, and self-government. But consider one case, the case of Joe Robertson, who actually was sent to prison for digging ponds on his own property. He ran afoul of the Federal Government because he dug *near* 'navigable waters' in order to supply water to Montana firefighters. How near? Well, the largest 'navigable body of water,' according to a common sense understanding of the phrase, that was close to Robertson was miles and *miles* away.

For his 'crime,' he went to prison for 18 months and had to pay $130,000 in 'restitution' which was deducted from his Social Security checks. He was 78 when he was sent to jail. He died shortly after his release, before his appeal could be heard. After his death, the courts threw out the whole thing. As well they should have, since everything about the case was a stench in the nostrils of any liberty-loving individual.

The "Clean Water Act," the cause of this monstrosity, was passed in the 1970's by people who probably would have insisted no such monstrosity could ever take place. Of course, almost all of those people are dead now. They do not have to face the consequences of their own actions. Moreover, the people who now enforce the law are not necessarily going to be the same kinds of people who passed it in the first place. To say that a certain fanaticism has overcome proponents of government oversight of the environment is an understatement, to say the least.

Just what is a 'navigable body of water'? As has been witnessed in the decades since, it means about whatever any government official thinks it means. So, to court they all go. Of course, if you are a government official, going to court means next to nothing, since the costs are underwritten by the Federal government with its bottomless wallet. The officials don't even actually go to court—the lawyers do that. For those harmed by the whims of the officials however, money is tight, and time is limited.

The CWA, like so many other Federal laws, helps illustrate everything said so far in this manifesto. We could talk about it at great length, which makes sense, since it has been talked about at great length for decades. For our purposes here, let us think of it in terms of its violation of the 'proximity' condition.

It is extremely difficult to see how Robertson's 'ponds' impacted any other 'body of water,' but even if it had, the people most likely able to determine that would have been his own neighbors. If Robertson or anyone else has a problem with the CWA, there is, practically speaking, nothing they can do about it. Their own towns, counties, and states can do nothing about it.

Getting rid of laws like this is like moving a mountain with a spoon.

Robertson's ponds apparently aided local firefighters. Let's say that there was some kind of discernible impact on some 'navigable water' on account of the ponds. Would this still be a problem? The local community may well reason that having water available to fight wildfires is more than enough to overlook some small amount of sludge trickling down a ditch. For every decision in life, there are trade-offs. The people most able to calculate the costs and benefits of most decisions are the ones making them, and the ones nearest to them.

To return to our forest management example, we can, for the sake of argument, envision a community wanting to forbid logging but not because they are eco-fanatics. Perhaps their community relies on tourism and outdoor sporting events, so having a wild landscape protected from large-scale harvesting of trees would make sense. But there will be communities who do not have the benefit of tourism and rely on the harvesting of trees to have an income—that is, to survive. Who is best able to calculate these tradeoffs? These individual communities, or state or Federal bureaucrats living hundreds or thousands of miles away?

In your mind's eye, you can see the honorable representative from Utah, where there are very few trees, reasoning to himself that survival income or not, the trees must be saved. He helps pass national legislation which authorizes bureaucrats in Washington DC to manage the lumber across the country. They say, "People who make their money selling logs will decimate our woodlands and so they *all* must be managed by the government!" There is a certain logic to it. The reality is often different.

For, as it happens, if you make your money selling logs, then you will be especially keen to make sure you always have logs to sell. You will know, better than most, how to establish new groves of trees, which trees to select-cut and which to leave, and so on. Counter-intuitively, the people the bureaucrats feared would harm the environment end up being the ones not only most suited for protecting the environment, but also the most motivated to do so. Unlike our dreamy bureaucrats longing for a forest utopia, our loggers are longing for food in their bellies and a roof over their heads.

It is not to say that there might not be a reason to be concerned about the loggers getting carried away. One might imagine loggers to be as inclined towards greed as any other human that has lived. But it is a false choice to say that this obviously means we need to make a Federal case out of it. There are other choices. There is the local community who can be involved, and if the matter transcends even that community, it could become the attention of the county. In such a scenario, our loggers can make their case directly to the people who are most affected, and the people who are most affected can make their case right back.

But if the loggers have to make their case about innumerable facets of their job which suddenly are managed by people thousands of miles away, the task becomes impossible. If, perchance, they have to close down their operations because they cannot comply with all of the regulations, don't want to risk going to a Federal prison if they violate them, they may very well descend into poverty. If they do, you can be quite sure that the honorable representative from Utah will never even be aware. The community which survived on the income from the logging industry, which then withers and dies because the loggers leave, never forgets.

I have used logging as a way to illustrate how these dynamics work and led with the case of Robertson being tread beneath the Clean Water Act to provide a real-world example of what does actually happen. Now imagine it isn't just the CWA, but thousands of other such laws, as well, applied to thousands of other industries.

And now recall that it is often the case that the well-connected and wealthy tend to be the beneficiaries of these laws, as they have the resources to have them written in a way that benefits them, whereas individuals do not. And if they do run afoul of the law, the chances are really good that with the right lawyer and a turn of circumstances, the plain reading of the text can be miraculously ignored, and the rich and connected get away with violating it completely.

The solution is not another Federal law or Supreme Court decisions 'clarifying' the laws. These are merely rearranging the chairs on the deck of the Titanic. The solution is to return to the only conditions which keep us from descending into chaos. Federal and state laws concerning things that are almost self-evidently best managed by local communities alone, accumulating and compounding, are a sure way to collapse a society. Just give it enough time.

The Fourth Condition that allows a civil society to exist and persist without relying on a tyrant's boot to keep the 'peace' is that the citizenry must not seek to take over the tyrant's job. Citizens must refrain from involving the government except along the narrow lines as described above, because to involve the government means to ultimately involve force. I ask you: just what is the difference between a tyrant imposing his will by force and a society passing laws and creating systems, backed by the coercive powers of the state, that can only be reversed—practically speaking—by the same mechanisms one might use to overthrow a tyrant?

Forget theory, what is the actual case? Never mind high-minded idealism, what is the actual net effect? The levers of power so established for proper governing can just as easily be abused, unless the citizens themselves stay their hands except in matters truly warranting the exercise of those powers.

In order for this to 'work,' one must be able to live with the fact that almost every other person in the world prefers to live their lives very differently than you. It is not merely possible, but actual, that everyone else orders priorities in a way that you don't. Even people who are like-minded will find, if they converse long enough, that there are things they disagree about. Of these arguments between both friend and foe, which of you would like to settle the argument by bringing a gun into the affair? For, in ultimate terms, that is precisely what having the government enforce a particular viewpoint *actually means*.

I ask again, which arguments warrant the use of force to settle them? Even this will be cause for dispute, hence the three prior conditions which strive to ensure that there will be a very narrow class of issues being settled via the government. The general rule should be that everyone should mind their own business and only get into the business of others where there is genuine friction between individuals or regions, and only at the level of government required to settle it. Apart from that, unless it be to save lives or secure their physical safety, no recourse to the government should be sought.

Note, I am not talking about the structure of the system, but the attitude of the people who would engage with that system. This whole 'there ought to be a law' mentality has got to go.

Because people have it so entrenched in their minds to resolve our most minute differences via the government, I have to repeat a previous point: just because I am asserting that we should not involve the government, it doesn't follow that people should do nothing. Almost everything that people would have the government do has, in the past, been done by individuals or local communities acting completely on their own.

This includes charity work, such as taking care of orphans and the homeless, and the impoverished. Indeed, In the United States, until the 1930's, individuals and communities took charge of helping those who needed help. Progressives at the time did not complain that there wasn't enough money being tasked for the benefit of the poor, but that the money being spent was being done so 'inefficiently.'

Your knee-jerk instinct is to say, "What is the problem with wanting to be efficient?" But one would do well to remember that the complaints were not about how the money was being managed, but on who the money was being directed at. It was the era of eugenics and compulsory sterilization, of Margaret Sanger's *The Pivot of Civilization*[10] and the Supreme

---

[10] In this book, Sanger has a whole chapter on the 'Cruelty of Charity,' by which she means it is cruel to keep certain poor people alive. Yes, she really meant that it would be better if they were dead so that they couldn't breed. This statement by Sanger in the book sums it up nicely:

"I realize as well as the most conservative moralist that humanity requires that healthy members of the race should make certain sacrifices to preserve from death those unfortunates who are born with hereditary taints. But there is a point at which philanthropy may become positively dysgenic, when charity is converted into injustice to the self-supporting citizen, into positive injury to the future of the race. Such a point, it seems obvious, is reached when the incurably defective are permitted to procreate and thus increase their numbers."

Court's decision, *Buck vs. Bell.*[11] Hear me: to the progressives of the early 1900's, 'charity' did not mean *helping* the poor, but *eliminating* the poor.[12] The transfer of 'benevolence' from individuals and local communities to Big Government proved to be tragic for many Americans in the early part of the 1900's, and examples continue to this present day. However, the transfer now complete, despite the damage continuing to be inflicted even as I write, good luck finding a remedy. It is hard enough getting the individual states to curtail their abuses and mitigate the unintended consequences. The Federalization of the bulk of it makes it nearly impossible to fix.

Progressives and their ilk have been instigators of many of the problems discussed to this point, but on the issue of charity and public order, 'conservatives' have been equally to blame. On the former, they find any argument for involving the government in charity irresistible if it is 'for the children' (nor can they

---

[11] In the words of Chief Justice Oliver Wendell Holmes, writing in the decision:

"It is better for all the world if, instead of waiting to execute degenerate offspring for crime or to let them starve for their imbecility, society can prevent those who are manifestly unfit from continuing their kind. The principle that sustains compulsory vaccination is broad enough to cover cutting the Fallopian tubes. Three generations of imbeciles are enough"

[12] The author DH Lawrence said this in 1908:

"If I had my way, I would build a lethal chamber as big as the Crystal Palace, with a military band playing softly, and a Cinematograph working brightly; then I'd go out in the back streets and main streets and bring them in, all the sick, the halt, and the maimed; I would lead them gently, and they would smile me a weary thanks; and the band would softly bubble out the 'Hallelujah Chorus'."

stomach being called 'uncompassionate' by political foes) and on the latter, they have found it impossible to keep their hands off of matters that don't impact them at all, but make them uncomfortable.

Examples abound, but of late we might point to the Federal law prohibiting the sale of tobacco products to those under the age of 21. In other words, one very large group of adults decided that another very large group of adults cannot use a legal product. 'Conservatives' had no problem with this, and this isn't even "for the children." People who can vote, are sent to war, and enter into life-altering contracts are imposed upon by this law.

Such measures are often imposed on sub-populations of fellow adults "for their own good" but proponents generally know just how paternalistic this argument comes across, even if it is a large part of their real reasons for advocating for such measures. They know how it sounds, and, they know in their hearts that it is paternalistic, but they like to think the best of themselves so they tell themselves whatever lies they need to justify whatever it is they are doing to their fellow man at any given point. Thus, the argument they raise publicly, rather than their *real* argument, also needs to be addressed here, which is that indeed these choices by their fellow adults do in fact impact us 'all.'

The argument is made that the use of tobacco (as just one example in the class of issues) is unhealthy and leads to society eventually paying large medical bills for long term tobacco users. Thus, because society is 'footing the bill', they feel that they have a right to decide how the money is spent. But how is it that society is 'footing the bill' in the first place? Who decided it was a good idea to have the tax-payers subsidize health care in the first place?

Ostensibly, paying for people's health care is an 'obvious good,' but this opens the door to the fact that literally every facet of human behavior becomes subject to political wrangling. How could it not? 'Health' care, by its very definition, potentially refers to every part of an individual's life, with no exception. There isn't anything that can't be seen through the prism of 'health,' whether it be mental health, physical health, spiritual health, population health, and so on and so forth. It is therefore inevitable that everything about an individual's life falls within the political arena at some point because, ya know, "society is footing the bill."[13]

Instead of people owning up to the consequences of their own actions, 'society' must take an interest because it is 'society' enduring the consequences. In places where they are positively drenched in this way of thinking, we see the entirely predictable results such as rationing.

In the United Kingdom, just a few years ago the National Health Service decided, on its own volition (that is, it was decided by bureaucrats, not a vote by

---

[13] There are particularly vile people out there who take advantage of this reality. They know that they can't get what they want directly, so instead they get the taxpayers to subsidize some element of it, and then they use the rationale that "society is paying for it" to get what they want—power and control over the lives of an unwilling populace—indirectly.

the public), to forbid treatment to people they, in their own sole discretion, had determined to be 'obese.' They also required people to give up smoking before getting treatment. In both cases, the NHS was not going to take anyone's word for it, but was going to back up their policy with required testing. This is justified on the basis that "Society has to pay for it!" Of course, the people being refused treatment are part of society, also pay taxes, and supposedly are entitled like the rest of their fellow citizens to 'free' health care.

Why stop at obesity and smoking? There is no particular reason why one shouldn't or couldn't keep going. This line of thinking can be logically extended to everything. The only recourse is a public outcry, such as the case where the NHS refused to prevent a man from going blind in one eye on the argument that he had another perfectly fine one.[14]

Surely health care wouldn't be denied to anyone based on their mere opinions, would they? In early 2020, the NHS ruled that people could be denied care if they were deemed 'racist' or 'sexist.' This seemed to be limited to the behavior of the patients when they presented for care, not because of social media posts or something they said in a tavern three years earlier, but when it's the NHS you are talking about, anything could be in the offing. The danger in this case is that in UK, like other places in the West these days, the bar is really low on what constitutes 'racism' or 'sexism.' It is so low, it is practically on the ground.

---

[14] Jack Tagg. This incident was back around 2008.

If I told my nurse that I liked my coffee black, you can be sure some of them would consider that to be 'abusive.' My mere stating of this will be considered 'racist.' It is the era of peanut butter and jelly sandwiches being regarded as 'racist,' so I find myself doubtful that the behavior the NHS was alarmed by actually was racist or sexist. Anyway, once you extend your reach into 'health,' you extend your reach into every nook and cranny of society. Civil society does not remain for long when every nook and cranny of each person's lives become subject to the political process.

Or what about the notorious Liverpool Care Pathway, where, to save money for the 'system,' they stopped feeding old people so that they would die faster? Ostensibly justified with the argument that the people were already dying, in practice, many of the people who died were relatively healthy—right up to the point where they decided to stop feeding them! This UK practice was disbanded and reformed a few years back, but helps make it clear that this is not a trifling matter. Take your eye off these people for one minute, and people literally die. And 'these people' theoretically are society's most educated, most sympathetic, most empathetic, most bleeding-hearted individuals. God save us if Republicans were in charge![15]

'Public outcry' is a far cry from self-government. Regardless of how noble your intentions are or sincere in your motives, once the government is involved, that

---

[15] I'm being facetious.

is the end of self-government. This is a veritable tautology, and yet most people don't understand it. We must understand it. We must dispense with our high-sounding plaudits about 'democracy' even as we create a myriad of fundamentally undemocratic institutions and bureaucracies. If you really value self-government and the 'consent of the governed' put your money where your mouth is and start minding your own business. You govern you; let your fellow man govern himself.[16]

The alternative, inevitably, is societal collapse. Eventually, some group does something to some other group which they find absolutely reprehensible. Being denied the ability to wriggle out from beneath the thumb of the first group, the second group acts in desperation. It accumulates and compounds. It 'works' until it doesn't.

The fifth condition: oversight. One of the great difficulties of flaunting all of the conditions described above is again one of pragmatics. The engorging of the various levels of government creates a situation where it is just not possible for citizens to know what is being done 'for' them. Are old people being killed off to save a buck? Many people would be outraged— if only they knew about it. Are the well-connected tapping into government grants using bribery and loopholes? Most people would be outraged—if only they knew about it. So on, and so forth.

---

[16] I repeat, this does not mean leaving the poor and needy completely to their own devices. This is a dishonest contention which I reject completely.

The common remedy for this dynamic is to create another committee to look after the other committees looking after the other committees providing oversight for the initial committee. Surely, the absurdity of this approach is apparent.

The problem of "who watches the watchers" always exists. The framers argued that the People were the ones who watch the watchers, but then, what they initially proposed was small enough and discrete enough that it was actually possible to do the watching. Not so, anymore. In fact, one does not need to create too many layers of agencies and bureaucracies before it is impossible for anyone to do the watching. And when the cat's away, the mice will play. Sometimes the mice will just try to enrich themselves. But sometimes the mice chip away at our liberties and freedoms without anyone being the wiser. Ten thousand mice later, we end up in chaos and disorder, wondering where all of our freedoms went.

The only way that our government works is if it truly is watched by the people. This is only possible if the government is small. Very small. Governments in America are, practically speaking, unwatchable. This is a recipe for disaster.

There are probably other conditions as well but let me close with **this sixth condition**: People need to be able to vote with their feet.

I heard someone say once that the glory of America is that in America, even the poor are rich. Relative to the rest of the world, this is definitely true. In that same spirit, one of the glories of America is that its refugees still have their possessions, freedoms, and liberties. If they find things not to their liking in one part of the country, they are free to move to another part of the country. Only their own comfort level and access to resources may restrict them. According to the Constitution, no state may prevent the free travel of the citizens of any other state through or within their state.

(Of late, we've seen even this law trampled on, haven't we? Be that as it may, we will continue to discuss this principle in the abstract.)

The founders had their own reasons for insisting upon this provision, but it is also vital to ensuring our republic 'works.' If a citizen believes that their city, county, or state has created a circumstance especially noxious, he has several avenues open to him before the option of violence is considered. He can work through the system to change the circumstances legally, for example. For this solution to work, the conditions discussed above need to be in place. He can learn to live with the odious situation. If the issue is sufficiently important to him, or worse, his fellow citizens continue to add to the offense, we are down to the two options we all know so well, *fight* or *flight*.

If *flight* is denied to him, you can be sure that trouble is brewing.

People will endure almost anything before turning to violence. The world is filled with displaced peoples and refugees who found their previous situation untenable. These people could have tried to stay and 'fight,' but concluded, for whatever reason, that their best option was to flee. Many times, the best option in the long run is to rise up and defeat whatever tyrant is causing the problem to begin with, but even setting aside considerations of resources, organization, and prospects for success, people are reluctant to actually kill. This is a good thing, although it is used against people by those with less scruples.

Thus, to keep the 'heat' down in our society, it must be possible for people, in a last resort, to change their locations peacefully. I suppose until recently no one thought that this principle was in danger of being ignored in the United States, but there are other ways to deny people the ability to 'change their locations.'

To illustrate, consider the monumentally high taxes and extremely intrusive laws that we witness in New York and California. These are so toxic to many of the states' citizens that they have despaired of conditions ever changing. Yet, having concluded that the conditions are foul, they also don't believe the conditions justify turning to force. Increasingly, however, many believe that the conditions justify getting out of their respective states as soon as humanly possible, which many proceed to do.[17]

---

[17] This has led to the complaint these newly 'displaced' citizens inexplicably keep advocating for the policies which drove them away from their previous homes. Having despoiled their old state, they now want to despoil their new state. This is going to create much resentment which should not be too easily dismissed. The problem can be solved easily enough: the 'refugees' must leave behind their dysfunctional ideology as well.

Now, the more intelligent of those creating these suffocating conditions know full well that they are driving people away. Do they think to themselves, "Selves, we've gone too far. Maybe we need to start rolling back our policies." ? No, of course not. Because, though intelligent, they lack the ability to introspect, or might even be outright malevolent. Their actual response is to hatch plans for taking their policies which were so distasteful to their own citizens that their citizens fled, and impose those policies on the entire nation. And if the entire nation is made to endure those policies, there is no place left to flee to; indeed, there is no point in fleeing at all.

They pat themselves on the back for this brilliant maneuver, complimenting themselves on their manner of 'progressively' improving the nation despite the many 'selfish' people who oppose their plans. (That's what they always call these people. If someone flees a place with oppressive taxes, they don't blame themselves for passing the oppressive taxes, they call the people who left 'selfish' and try to shame them.) In fact, it is another brick in the wall of tyranny. For, if one cannot escape California by fleeing to Missouri, there will eventually come a point where people do indeed conclude that there is no point in fleeing at all. Left with only one option... violence... it will be to violence that they then turn.

Thus, a radically diffused governance also defuses tensions. Our 'brilliant' political tacticians assume that they can play this game forever because they take for granted the acquiescence of the people when the chips are down. This is a grave miscalculation. When the people can no longer escape the greedy, groping fat fingers of the statist, the moment will have arrived. Things are a bit worse than what I have said so far. Not only is it the case that we are running out of places to go within the country, there are fewer and fewer countries that we could go to even if it proved necessary. All are on the same track. But that is a different topic.

Conditions, conclusion.

Pre-*after* readers may find the above to be absurd and hyperbolic. Maybe.

As I write, many Americans are chafing at the fact that there are still innumerable society-wide restrictions months and months after a 'pandemic' has undeniably already done its worse. Many Americans watched with horror as governors and mayors employed an American version of the Liverpool Care Pathway, sacrificing older people in order to ensure there were available resources for everyone else; this, in the face of an abundant amount of resources which never came close to being overwhelmed, except in very small areas of the country and for very short amounts of time.[18] Many Americans have watched as the unimaginable (to them) happened: tens of millions of people were literally confined to their homes; businesses were shuttered; travel restricted to a

---

[18] A good example would be the King of Bleeding-Hearts, Governor Cuomo (Democrat), who sacrificed thousands of elderly New Yorkers on the altar of 'managing scarce resources.'

standstill, even locally; food shortages were imminent, even as food was thrown away by the ton. Where there is discussion about a vaccine, there is also discussion about making it compulsory. In the same breath we hear that vaccines typically take years to create and test for efficacy and safety, we hear that we will, as a nation, have to be locked down until we have a vaccine.[19]

So, maybe many more pre-*after* readers will recognize how precarious things are than they were even a year ago. I suspect, however, that few post-*after* readers will find what has been written so far to be outlandish at all.[20]

Principles Applied

As interesting as it would be to contemplate how to start from scratch and build a new country on solid principles, it is impossible to know exactly what our

---

[19] Come on, admit it. We all know they are going to make that sucker compulsory or die trying. *We know it*. Or is it, "or kill trying"? Everything seems to be on the table these days.

[20] We will say a few more words about the handling of the 'pandemic' in what follows, but in actuality, the astute reader will see that what has already been said can be easily related to it. It is entirely plausible that the 'pandemic' will be a catalyst for bringing things to a head, but it is equally plausible that things will just plodding along. I have endeavored, as much as possible, to keep this document from being time-bound to my own contemporary situation, as I firmly believe the principles discussed herein are timeless. Events help to illustrate those principles, but when those events occur, whether it be in 1,000 BC or 3,000 AD, is irrelevant. So long as human nature is what it is, these principles will apply. (This is understood by the Conditioners, who have resolved to deal with these problems by altering human nature. Except to say that this is not within their power, I shall refrain from saying more about it at this time.)

starting parameters would actually be. No matter what happens, there will be a great deal of baggage to deal with. The only thing I'm confident of is that no one is going to be concerned about the arbitrary application of the Clean Water Act! Most of the Federal code will probably go out the window as America shatters into so many shards of glass, and much state law with it. I will probably make some comments along the 'start from scratch' line, but only because I can't help myself. I will focus, as I said at the beginning, on the vain attempt to smuggle these principles back into the republic so that there is not, God willing, an *after*.

Let me offer yet another way of presenting the principles above which might help us see how to recover the ground lost by the Constitution. What does it look like to have a limited government along the lines that the framers sought? I think it might look like this: our goal should be that politicians cannot possibly be construed as heroes.

It is bizarre, really, that people whose primary work is to spend other people's money ever inspire enthusiasm or that we would want them to. It is insane, really, that politicians would be given legal access to the most intimate affairs of the population, regardless of whether or not they avail themselves of that access. Certainly, because of the width and breadth of what the President of the United States can actually do (almost anything he or she wants), it makes sense that we would perceive the President to be a leader. It makes sense that our presidential campaigns would become super-heated since the person we elect will be heavily imprinted into our most private affairs. What doesn't make sense is that we would ever allow anyone to have that power in the first place.

And why should there be 'leaders' in a republic, anyway? We give lip service to the idea that our 'leaders' are democratically elected, but if the power belongs to the people, we should be looking for our leaders from among the people. The 'leaders' become administrators of the will of the people. Administrators are not known for being especially heroic.

If powers were stripped from our politicians, less would hang in the balance when we elected them. There would, consequently, be less heat associated with our political process. These things go together and cannot be separated. People who bemoan how our society is becoming fractured and fanned into flames, who do not understand that the principal reason this is happening is because our politicians are fighting over the management of our entire lives, are like people who complain about their house burning down even as they are throwing gasoline into the structure. Certainly, a house can still burn without the gasoline, but it's a lot easier to put out a fire if no fuel is being added while we are trying to extinguish it.

Having invoked fire-fighting, let us consider who the heroes really are. They are the people who face physical danger so that we don't have to. It is the fire-fighter, the police officer, and the soldier. The heroes are the ones that rush into the jaws of death—

literally—to save as many as they can. Real heroes often die because of their actions. If a politician or bureaucrat dies, its likely because of old age or a car accident.

Real heroes are the average citizens who take the initiative in their own homes and communities to stand up to pressure of the mob. Real heroes spend their own money for the common good. The sacrifice is their own. They do not go around taking money from their neighbors by force and then stand in the public square distributing what they've taken, expecting and receiving praise from their fellow citizens.

Don't get me wrong. At present, there are plenty of real heroes in our political system. My point is that if our political system requires heroism, there is something wrong with our political system. Our goal should be to make it so that being a politician is such a boring, mundane job, nobody actually wants it.

In fact, it is already the case that the people that we'd most want to be politicians have no interest in the job. I heard it said once that you can be sure that any man interested in the job of being the President of the United States is a man you would not want anywhere near the position. This certainly does seem to be the case. Unfortunately, we don't seem to have any other options. The more decent candidates are quickly eliminated. The really best people never try at all.

If you are reading this before *after*, what I'm saying may seem impractically difficult to obtain. I remind you, this document is not written with you today in mind, but you, *after*. The *After*-You must seek to rebuild our political system which does not contain the seeds of its own destruction. That means not putting so much weight on the outcome of our elections. The *After*-You sees the wisdom of this.

How, then in the interim, shall we proceed? I will sketch out some specific ideas, now. Please note that these are educated suggestions which I think might work, offered in the spirit of sparking a conversation among those who see the need to act decisively to save the republic. I have other ideas I chose not to share in this document, waiting for that future conversation. Other people might have some other ideas. The important thing is to start the conversation among a large enough group of people for it to matter.

In what follows, it should be noted that each proposal assumes that all the other proposals have all likewise been adopted. Whether or not this is necessary for the country to be restored can be debated, but in my estimation, we need all of them at once.

Let us first acknowledge that the checks and balances built into the US Constitution have *not* worked. They were not robust enough. The founders themselves skirted them at their earliest opportunity. We must introduce new checks and balances and refresh some of the existing ones.

Recall the words of the Declaration of Independence: "whenever any Form of Government becomes destructive of these ends, it is the Right of the People to alter or to abolish it, and to institute new Government."

"The People" are. at least on paper, the final check on government abuse. Earlier I quoted James Madison. Immediately after his statement which I quoted above, he said, "A dependence on the people is, no doubt, the primary control on the government; but experience has taught mankind the necessity of auxiliary precautions."

Experience has taught us that our framers' auxiliary precautions were not sufficient. I submit that instead of only giving lip service to 'The People' as a check, we put our money where our mouth is.

In retrospect, we can see that it was most wise for certain framers to insist on a Bill of Rights, even though theoretically it was redundant in light of the actual writing of the Constitution. The inclusion of the 2nd Amendment was clutch, as the 'right to bear arms' helps show that the framers were not kidding about what they saw as the ultimate means of preventing the government from going crazy.

However, without spelling out explicitly when and how the People can legitimately and appropriately execute their judgement that the government needed to be replaced by force, it effectively rendered the amendment impotent. Most people are peace-loving, law-abiding folks, and are willing to put up with quite a bit before, backed into a corner, they are inclined to 'fight.' Without clear language telling them when it is appropriate to act, they won't.

(1) Enforcement Amendment

I propose that we remedy this by providing that clear language. Something like this:

> Whenever the People have determined that their own government has flagrantly disregarded the principles and values of the Constitution over a period of time, and other methods to restrain or reform the government have failed, they may call for and promptly obtain a referendum of the People, through an orderly process facilitated by their elected officials if possible, but through direct action if necessary.
>
> If 2/3rds of the people voting support the removal of the government, the People may muster in whatever number that they so choose, organized in any fashion that they deem appropriate, armed with whatever weapons they desire, and then proceed to remove the offending individuals by force, if these same refuse to relent, or resign. These, and those which attempt to defend them, if they refuse to relent or resign, shall consider their lives forfeit.
>
> Every level of government—any entity with any access to police powers—within the United States, from the smallest township to the city, to the state, or the Federal government itself, may be so removed.
>
> In addition to the right to call for and obtain

a referendum, such a referendum shall also be held every two years, during the same election in which Federal representatives are elected. A line shall be included for each jurisdiction and sub-jurisdiction each citizen resides within, so that each citizen may cast a vote pertaining to every level of police power exerted against him. His vote may only count towards the population he is within the jurisdiction of, and if in some other jurisdiction a 2/3rds vote has been obtained, no other citizen or government may obstruct their removal of the offending agents or agencies, lest their lives be forfeit.

In the bi-annual referendums, the 2/3rds rule shall only be enforceable by the people if there also is a turnout of at least 51% of the adult population who cast a vote in the referendum.

In any referendum, the refusal of other citizens to vote shall not be construed as a vote for or against the referendum, and instead such citizens shall be considered indifferent as to the outcome.

Any attempt by any government official at any jurisdiction to oppose this process or obstruct the enforcement of the results of the 2/3rds vote shall be met with their swift removal by The People by whatever means the People deem necessary.

The People are understood only to be those

legal citizens within the jurisdiction of the United States, being at least 18 years of age.

I believe an amendment like this which provides not just the authorization to remove the abusive government but also lays out a mechanism for proceeding may, all by itself, compel our elected officials to be more cautious in their execution of their offices. It is a last resort but at least there is one.

Preferably, no politician or bureaucrat would ever feel inclined to test the patience of the People. To help give the political class a head's up, as it were, to the true sentiments of the people (if the results of the bi-annual referendum isn't enough!), another amendment would require the inclusion of a ballot item indicating whether or not the people consent to be governed.

Here is an irony. Allegedly, our government governs on the basis of the consent to be governed. However, in my nearly five decades of life so far, I have never once been asked if I consent to be governed. None of us have. More than that, what mechanism have I been offered to show that I withdraw my consent? None.

I have heard it said that my mere participation in our electoral process indicates my consent. This is strange, since the same people I've heard say that also advocate for making voting compulsory. How these two things can be reconciled, I can't imagine. Naturally, they are so oblivious to logic and reality that it has not even occurred to them that they are mouthing a contradiction. Allow me to do their thinking for them, then, and ask the obvious: "How precisely may I give my consent to be governed and how precisely may I remove it?"

(2) Consent Amendment

We may follow the same pattern as the above amendment, by allowing citizens to call for and obtain a referendum regarding consent and by having bi-annual items on the election ballots indicating whether or not there is consent to be governed. **I propose** that the 'consent' amendment might then say:

> The People may call for and obtain a referendum through an orderly process facilitated by their elected officials if possible, but through direct action if necessary, which specifies the following two ballot items:
>
> 1. I give my consent to be governed.
> 2. I withdraw my consent to be governed.

In addition to the right to call for and obtain a referendum at any time, such a referendum shall also be held every two years, during the same election in which Federal representatives are elected. A line shall be included for each election in each jurisdiction and sub-jurisdiction each citizen resides within, so that each citizen may cast a vote pertaining to every level of police power exerted against him. His vote may only count towards the population for which he is within the jurisdiction.

Upon any result in which 2/3rds of the votes cast in a jurisdiction indicate that they withdraw their consent, the government of that jurisdiction must then resign upon the certification of the vote, and a convention shall be called within that jurisdiction to seek and obtain the satisfaction of The People. The convention shall have the power to institute a temporary governance in order to maintain law and order but any temporary measure so instituted will expire immediately after 120 days of the inauguration of the convention have passed. The newly formulated government crafted by the convention shall promptly be submitted to the jurisdiction for a vote. A 2/3rds affirmation by the people of the jurisdiction shall legitimize the new government.

Any attempt by any government official at any jurisdiction to oppose this process or obstruct the enforcement of the results of the 2/3rds vote shall be met with their swift removal by The People.

Both of these amendments require a laborious effort and leaping high hurdles, and that is on purpose. The progressives desire a strong central government and a strong central 'leader' so that they can implement whatever they want, quickly. However, it is precisely the many obstacles and time-consuming processes which help to secure freedom and liberty.

Contrary to the assertions of the progressives, it is not necessarily the case that others, including 'conservatives', are opposed to all changes to society. What non-progressives desire, however, is that the changes are carefully considered and carefully implemented and unintentional consequences taken into account. The bigger the change to the larger population, the more time should be taken to implement it. And, obviously, the change should be made on the 'up and up,' and not through judicial *fiat* or procedural maneuvers, and so on. The People must be on board.

With the same idea in mind, I do not think it wise to make it an easy process to "to alter or to abolish" a government which has turned destructive. Nor should it be an easy call for a convention. However, it should not be practically impossible, either. That is the case now. At present, there is a way to change the Constitution but not a way that the People can do so without going through intermediaries. Moreover, a simple majority cannot be enough to move such monumental measures forward.

In my thinking, the referendum for directly removing officials and the referendum on indicating consent or lack thereof, provide real-time information for everyone to see just where the People stand. While it is not plausible that a politician would be elected with 51% of the vote and simultaneously 67% of the population call for his removal, by force if necessary, it is plausible that a politician could be elected with 51% of the vote but 60% of the people vote to withdraw their consent.

60% is not enough to force a convention, but it should be enough to let the politician know he should be very careful to govern according to the rules. That 60% also informs the community that they are not 'crazy' or uniquely 'selfish.' Whatever else the media might say or what not, such a high number tells everyone that something stinks and it is in everyone's interests to get things fixed, fast. For, it is fairly clear that any population leaning more and more towards withdrawing their consent is likewise leaning more and more towards using force to deal with the problem directly.

Observe that I indicate that each election would have an option added regarding consent. So, even the election of the local mayor might have this for the ballot items:

> For Mayor of Town Z:
> [ ] Margaret Munson
> [ ] Paul Seltzer
> [ ] I do not consent to be governed
>   by either of these candidates.

As it stands, our current ballot system forces us to choose between candidates that many of believe are equally odious. By not having an option to not elect *either* candidate, the message is that it would be worse to have an office go unfilled than to have a scoundrel fill it. In the same vein, if the turnout is poor, this could very well be because no one likes either candidate. To hear people talk, however, you have a duty to vote no matter what. That is, your lack of voting is construed as not participating in civil society, rather than registering your contempt for the candidates; you are told you deserve whatever you get if you chose not to vote.

I think having the office unfilled is a perfectly acceptable option for people to weigh in on. If things go on merrily with the position unfilled, people may get the idea that the position wasn't that important to begin with. I think that would be a good thing. If people decide that having the position unfilled leads to unacceptable problems, they can either suck it up and vote for one of the people they rejected before, or maybe they can go back to the drawing board on a quest for resolving those problems. Maybe they will dissolve the office and find some other way to resolve the problem. Maybe they will fill it and never withdraw their consent again.

Regardless, the current system merely extends the *status quo*. The *status quo* is the problem. The opportunity to withdraw consent, being built right into the system, likewise builds into the system the opportunity to reform and revise the government on a regular basis. That is just what the doctor ordered.

Are these amendments the best way forward? I don't know for sure. Remember, I'm trying to get something going within the existing Constitutional framework so as to save the republic. If I was starting from scratch, maybe I'd propose something different. Continue to bear that in mind as I offer even more ways to introduce checks and balances to a system which is steadily eroding the ones we already have.

The original Constitution carved out a very important role for the individual states. Indeed, the mechanisms for amending the Constitution came through the assent of the states. The states were able to keep the Federal government in check by having their own representatives—the senators. Originally, these were appointed by the legislatures of the states. The Constitution was amended in the early 1900s to provide for direct election of senators. This was a grave mistake and marks a big erosion of our system of checks and balances. The institution of the Senate was designed to prevent Federal overreach at the expense of the states. Now, however, this check is gone.

(3) Repeal of 17th Amendment

I hereby propose that once again, senators are selected by their respective states. However, the various states should also be compelled to provide a mechanism for the recall of senators who cease to serve the interests of their state. This will provide another way, outside of the use of force, by which the Federal government can be brought to heel. If the individual states believe, in sufficient numbers, that the Federal authority goes too far, they will have their own representatives who can throw cold water on the overreach.

That said, it is very clear to me that the states are themselves too big, and in their own way, confined to their own jurisdictions, have become veritable 'Feds' with their overreach. So, even if the states once again had their own representation, it is doubtful that the states would be able to keep the Feds in check, or keep themselves in check. It is also inevitable that the people the states choose as their representatives aren't really representative of a very large number of people in the state.

I asked before what California had to do with Kentucky. We could just as easily ask, "What does Cook county have to do with Madison county?" I refer to two counties in the state of Illinois. Chicago is in Cook county and has a population by itself of more than 5,000,000 people, whereas Madison county only has 230,000 people in it, and is on the opposite side of the state. This lop-sided arrangement pretty well ensures that the people of Madison county are nothing more than a piggy bank for the people of Chicago, which, if anyone is familiar with the state of finances in Illinois, is not really an exaggeration.

The 5,000,000 people of the Chicago area rival in population the entire population of the state of Wisconsin which is right next to it. One might say that the people of the Chicago area have out-sized influence at the state level but under-sized influence at the Federal level. I'm not sure how important such distinctions are, but it does speak to whether or not self-government is real. The people of Chicago have the ability to do just about anything they want to everybody else in the state, *and they have.*

Such tensions exist throughout the country.

In Wisconsin, the city of Milwaukee, population 600,000 has no shared interests (from the perspective of justified reasons to involve the arbitration of a government) with the people of Iron county, population 6,000. The people of Milwaukee should not be held to the whims of people nearly three hundred miles away. By the same token, the people in Iron county should not be ruled by people three hundred miles away with concerns related to life together in close proximity.

Don't get us started on New York City versus the rest of the state!

There is a reason why in some places, most notably, the state of California, there is constant chafing to divide up their states into several states. The reasons are similar to ones I've stated so far, such as the impracticality of governing justly from so far away, the divergent values of people living entirely different lives and the lack of a common basis requiring shared governing, and so on.

(4) Amendment to Create 'Protectorates'

I therefore propose the creation of something like 'mini-states.'

We do not want to see a balkanization of the United States,[21] but it appears to me that to maintain a civil society, we need another 'layer' between the state

---

[21] Or, should I say, not any more balkanization. It is already in progress.

governments and the counties. This layer should be as the states are now. That is, these layers should have their own representatives, their own senators, and so on. As I imagine them, they are so much like states that I am tempted simply to call them states, and be done with it. However, after much thought, I have concluded that to help maintain continuity with the United States as presently constituted, I have opted to leave the states as states, and call these new layers, "protectorates."

This is not very catchy, but seems to be the best existing term to cover what I am proposing.

The Wikipedia entry on the term, for whatever that is worth, is:

> A protectorate … is a dependent territory that has been granted local autonomy and some independence while still recognizing the suzerainty of a greater sovereign state. In exchange for this, the protectorate usually accepts specified obligations, which may vary greatly, depending on the real nature of their relationship. Therefore, a protectorate is an autonomous area under a higher sovereignty.

The difference between this and what I'm proposing is that while allowing these newly formed 'protectorates' to remain under the 'protection' of their 'sovereign state,' the 'protectorates' themselves have rights before the Federal government, as though they also were states.

The protectorates should be created based on population size and geographic proximity but unlike states, can have borders that shift on a regular basis. Every ten years, such as is the case with re-districting the states, makes sense to me. A protectorate should not be allowed to exceed 1.5 million people in size. If it reaches that size, it should form two protectorates out of the one.

Further protections to citizens from their own governments would be secured by allowing counties to disassociate from one protectorate and connect to another. Within the counties, townships would have the right to disassociate from the county they are in and associate with a different county.

This probably sounds to the reader like a big mess, and it is. On the other hand, civil wars aren't cool, either. Conflicts occur when people are forced to submit to things they do not agree with and they have no way of reconciling those disagreements besides with force. By reducing the number of issues resolved via government and leaving the most important issues to the people themselves, and giving people the ability, through a known, orderly process, to escape being imposed upon, the causes of and severity of conflicts will be diminished.

Above, I insisted that states be compelled to provide a mechanism for recalling their senators. **I propose** that this mechanism come through the democratically expressed will of the individual protectorates. I suspect that most protectorates would end up patterning themselves like the states, themselves, with a governor, a house and senate, and a judiciary. Such a framework would prevent wanton disruption of the state's legitimate operations and oversight of the US senators. However, it would provide a 'relief valve' for the protectorates, as, at the very least, they would be able to express their firm disapproval when their US senators flaunt the interests of their constituents.

I think it is important that the protectorates be able to design their own system of government, but I would strongly recommend a republican form of government. Realistically, most people do not have the time, energy, or inclination to involve themselves in the affairs of the government. Direct democracy is rarely practiced in the United States, or anywhere else, for that matter, and for good reason. You do not have, for example, the affairs of the city managed and run on a day to day basis by the entire population of the city. No, they elect assemblymen, trustees, or mayors, who are then empowered to provide that management.

However much the larger part of the population prefers to just live their lives and leave the governing to others, there is no question that this deference by the population has been used against them. Whether it be at the level of the city, county, the state, the Federal government, or our newly formed protectorates, you can expect that this deference will persist. Given enough time, eventually the bloated overreach of the government will reach a tipping point, and we will once again have someone like myself penning a document pondering what to do *after*.

This sad assessment seems to me to be undeniably true. People just do not learn the lessons of history. If they don't see the damage themselves, they figure the threat must be overblown. They are so immersed in the affairs of their own daily lives that they don't understand that their deference today means tumultuous times for their children or grandchildren. Can we postpone this inevitable process, so that the tumultuous times are visited upon the great- or great-great grandchildren instead?

(5) A 'proximity' amendment to put a hard limit on government overreach

I think we can. We do it by enshrining a new bedrock principle: *governmental action is only permitted at the level of the individuals impacted.* The more intrusive the measures, the closer to the individual must be to the government implementing those measures, so that the individual has a practical chance to do something about it.

I hereby propose the following amendment:

> No governmental body, whether it be municipality or even the Congress of the United States, may enact *any* policy *whatsoever* which only concerns a population already represented by a lower governmental body, unless the lower governmental body directly concerning that population explicitly and voluntarily allows

for an exception. The lower governmental bodies have the absolute right to withdraw from arrangements in which they entered into in the first place voluntarily.

If a matter concerns only ten houses on a block, then the mayor of the city is precluded from enacting any policy whatsoever. The matter must be something that is directly applicable to the whole city, or else the mayor is precluded from acting. If a matter only concerns a single city, the county must mind its own business. If a matter only concerns a county, the protectorate must keep its hands off. If a matter is only relevant to a protectorate, the state must stay out of it. If a matter is only directly connected to a state, and not the nation as a whole, then the Federal government must keep the hell out of it.

Notice that this proposed amendment does not contain an enforcement provision. That is because I believe my other proposed amendments so far contain the necessary 'checks' on abuse.

Recognizing that a community may very well prefer to have certain issues managed by a higher level of government, the amendment specifically carves out a way for this to be accomplished. This would no doubt lead to a patchwork of confusing applications of the various levels of authority in the country, but when the alternative is death squads, I personally find it preferable.

If you don't know why it would be confusing, you haven't grasped what I'm proposing. Let me explain with a hypothetical. Let's say that Congress wants to pass a law establishing universal health care. On its face, this law blows the amendment out of the water. However, people who abhor the idea of such a program need not invoke the 'consent amendment' because there is a way to exclude themselves.

First, for such a program to become law, the senators will have to have voted for it. If the senators are appointed by the states and are not directly elected, the approval of the senate assures that the various states, as states, don't find the idea noxious. If the protectorates likewise have senators, their approval does the same. But this still does not make it applicable to every American. No. Since health care is something that can be obtained locally, a county, if it so desires, can refuse to participate in the program. If a township within the county resents not being able to participate in the program, it has the ability to associate itself with a county that *is* willing to participate in the program. And so it goes, right on up the chain through the counties, protectorates, and the states.

Thus, you could have a national program which slightly less than half of the country is not participating in. This may be something you find absurd, but if so, you must not have been paying very close attention during the rise of the Tea Party in 2010. The Obama administration rammed through his quasi-national health care program, getting zero Republican votes for the final product. That he could not get bi-partisan support should have been a clue that much of the country definitely did not want his program, but he went ahead with it anyway. The result was an epic smackdown of the Democrats throughout the country and a rise in hostilities among Americans ever since. I suppose Obama considered that to be worth it, but my opinion is that this is a price too high to pay. Looking back *after*, I bet many other Americans agree with me.

Authority You Can't Reclaim is Not *Actually* Delegated; It is Authority You Do Not Have at All!

There is an underlying principle which I have not yet dealt with directly. Simply put, it's the principle that, part and parcel to the idea of governing by the consent of the governed, is the notion that what those governing are really doing is exercising power delegated to it by the People. In this amendment, I am making this principle explicit. *But power delegated must be power that can be reclaimed.* If it cannot be reclaimed, then it is *not* power *delegated*, it is *not* governing by the consent of the governed. It is, at best, soft tyranny. I hope those reading this have not and never see what it is at the worst.

Incidentally, as a general statement, the various governments already have the power to use discretion so as to make nearly all of the programs they've established to be voluntary. We have government programs which we do not compel all Americans to participate in, although, granted, we make all Americans pay for them.

Something like health care could just as easily have been something which people had the option of signing on to, quite apart from geographic considerations. The argument was that the program would not work unless everyone participated, which was your first sign that the program would not work. Seeing all the troubles that government healthcare programs have had around the world, whether it be the rationing or the massive deficits, it's pretty clear by now that what they all have in common is that they are *run by the government* and *do not work*. At least, not without seriously trampling on the rights and liberties of the very people supposedly benefiting from the programs.

Perhaps you disagree. Nonetheless, many Americans had this belief and did not appreciate having your viewpoint summarily imposed on them, with little to no recourse. This put additional fuel on an already combustible mess. By 'this' I don't mean the imposition of Obamacare. I mean the "with little to no recourse" part. It is most unwise to continue along the same track. The ideas I have proposed so far aim to remove fuel from the fire. If, perchance, you are starting over, *after*, you should remember this principle well.

Much of the problem arises from the accumulation and compounding of law upon law, agency upon agency, bureaucracy upon bureaucracy, court decision upon court decision. If we presume that some law passed decades ago was passed in good faith and genuinely represented the legitimate delegation of powers from the citizens to the government on some matter, we are still left with the awkward fact that many, if not most, if not *all* of the people who did this delegation are long dead. Few, if any, of those alive now who endure or ostensibly benefit from that delegation have been given the opportunity to register their own opinion on the matter.

To take just one example out of many, consider Social Security. The general feeling as I write is that most people like Social Security and would like to keep it. These tend to be older folks who have been paying into the system for decades and are poised to begin receiving their own money back as they retire.[22] There is one problem: many others, in particular people my age and younger (and I am middle-aged as I write this), do not expect to get a dime from Social Security. As with all well-intentioned government programs, it was mismanaged from the beginning, built on precarious assumptions, fraught with corruption, and is now almost broke.

The estimates for when exactly Social Security will run out of money change periodically, but most of those estimates are in the 2020's to 2030's, which could either be tomorrow or fifteen years from now. I suspect that everyone figures that it doesn't matter

---

[22] A misconception that is actually part of the problem. Their money was not held for them, but was paid out to previous beneficiaries. The money they receive today is not their own, but money pulled from workers today. It is basically a big pyramid scheme. This scheme was created in the 1930s, when the population of the United States was about 130,000,000. The population of the US is now about 350,000,000 with a falling birth rate. This means that there will soon be more people demanding "their own money" but fewer people working to generate the cash flow to pay them.

much, as the pressure to 'bail out' the program will be so great that they'll make it happen even if it means going even further into debt. This will be a neat trick, as our current national debt is approaching 30 *trillion* dollars, with our unfunded liabilities totaling more than 150 *trillion* dollars. I further suspect that the significance of these numbers will be more obvious *after* than they are now.

At any rate, if I was asked if I wanted to create a new Federal retirement program right now, I would adamantly oppose it. I believe that Social Security should be disbanded and some way found to make whole those who bought into the idea that they were 'paying into' their own savings account. I would much prefer to manage my own money, thank you very much, especially when I'm reasonably confident that whatever money I give to the Feds to manage on my behalf, won't be there when it is finally my 'turn.' Even if it is there, it almost certainly won't be there for my children.

I am not the only one to think this. Have any of us dissenters been asked if we want to continue the program? Are we given the choice to not participate? You wish!

Now, to Social Security add the innumerable other laws passed since the nation's inception, at the state and Federal level. Add to it all the other programs where my opinion was not sought and my representatives did not address anew. Can we really say that these programs exist by the consent of the governed? No. At best they exist by the consent of those who died long ago. *My* consent was never sought or obtained.

(6) Amendment to Make All Legislation Expire after 25 Years

I submit that this dynamic is also part of the problem **so I therefore propose** the following amendment:

All laws passed, at any governmental level, expire after 25 years, with no exception. They may be renewed, but it must be by the regular legislative process which is required for the passage of all new laws.

Laws may be provided 'sunset clauses' which provide for an even earlier expiration, but must never provide a clause that extends the law beyond 25 years.

All laws in effect at the time this amendment comes into force have a grace period of ten years in which they remain in effect. Upon the conclusion of the ten years, if regular legislative action has not occurred to pass them anew, immediately expire.

Violations of this amendment, whether in the crafting and passage of the laws or by enforcement by executive branches, or any other agent of the government, shall be construed as willful defiance of the Constitution and shall initiate an immediate impeachment of those offending, or their prompt removal. Failure to address such insubordination by the appropriate authorities shall be remedied by the People, according to whatever fashion they decide is appropriate.

Legislation cannot be renewed except by the legislators in office in the two years prior to the statutory expiration of the laws.

A 25-year time horizon on every law passed will accomplish many things. In the first place, it will address the most fundamental problem of all, which is that it guarantees that no law will ever be in place for very long without the 'consent of the governed' being genuinely obtained. In the second place, as a derivative of the first, any law renewed will by necessity reflect current realities. The world can change a great deal in a very short amount of time. What seemed good at one time may seem wholly inappropriate two decades later. Thirdly, it will ensure that only the matters most appropriate for government involvement will be acted upon. The regular legislative process is an intentionally cumbersome process. Few are going to want to invest time and energy on matters that are relatively trivial if they know they will simply expire if presented to a future legislative body. This will have the effect, all by itself, of reducing the size and scope of the legislation in force and the legislation considered.

I suppose the reader believes this will result in the inevitable disappearance of many 'improvements' to our country, all the more so if the reader is a progressive, who doesn't believe an improvement has occurred unless a multi-billion dollar program has been created, at tax-payer expense, which is compulsory and backed by the coercive powers of the state. And yet the amendment I have proposed plainly states that laws can be renewed. If a law is genuinely an 'improvement,' those living a generation hence will obviously agree, and will renew the legislation.

I would ask those who chafe at this amendment how fair they consider it that people who are not even born yet will be forced to submit to the laws we find important, today. The current system essentially establishes the rule of future citizens by the citizens who came before them. That is, it is chronological totalitarianism. The accumulation of laws, over time, encompass more and more of our being, such that future citizens cannot, as a practical matter, possibly unravel all of the various impositions upon them. The Federal code itself is thousands and thousands and thousands of pages thick. Self-government by future citizens simply is not practically possible... unless these laws are regularly and intentionally brought up for review and allowed to expire if later generations deem them not important enough to renew.

The amendment as proposed encompasses every legislative body, and therefore by extension (in a sane universe), all regulation and executive orders, whether it be the mayor of a small town or the governance of a state. The principle becomes even more important as legislation becomes ever more intrusive on one's daily lives, which, if my principles be put into practice, are going to be the laws passed by their own local municipalities, counties, and protectorates. It therefore is necessary to have the amendment apply to them as well, and ensures that no law passed by one generation will not be renewed again without the generation just being born when it was initially passed having at least seven years of adulthood to revise, refresh, or revoke the law.

Speaking of our national deficit. The chances are very good that whatever our *after* looks like, it will have been caused by or exacerbated by the massive debt that our country is in at every level. The debt by the Federal government, the states and municipalities, and even the citizens, is unsustainable. I look into our future and I see Zimbabwe, Venezuela, or even the Weimar Republic. I hope I'm wrong, but I don't know how I could be. I guess we'll see.

At any rate, the cause of this massive debt can be traced to two basic things.

One, the Sixteenth amendment, which dispensed with taxation being "apportioned among the states" and gave the Federal government the right to directly tax individuals, wherever they were in the country, however they earned their money, and, well, in whatever way they pleased.

Secondly, the establishment of the Federal Reserve. The Constitution expressly gave the management of our country's money supply to Congress. Not, I should add, to the president or the judiciary. In other words, the management of our money was supposed to be performed by those directly accountable to the people. The Federal Reserve, despite its misleading name, is a private organization which is ultimately run with an eye towards profit by individuals most of us will never even know about. The oversight provided by Congress is token. Thankfully, the investors of the Federal Reserve know what side of their bread is buttered, so they work hard to keep our politicians happy, so the policies of the Federal Reserve are not too egregious.

Still, the way the Federal Reserve earns its income is the same as the way all banks earn money, and that is by lending money and charging interest on that money. Obviously, the more money leant, the more interest earned. Thus, the Federal Reserve, by its very nature, is going to be very open to the idea of the United States taking out loan after loan, by the billions and trillions. There is no incentive for the Federal Reserve to restrain the drunken sailor posture of our country, except insofar as ensuring that the country doesn't act so recklessly as to make it insolvent. That is, so recklessly as to be unable to make the interest payments.

Where does the money come from to make these payments? The tax-payers. With Congress effectively turning over matters to the executive branch and the Federal Reserve, this is yet another variation on the 'taxation without representation' problem.

How to resolve this problem?

Once again, the Constitution did not quite provide the necessary checks and balances to prevent abuse of our money supply. However, I guess we should be happy that they did us compliment of passing an actual Constitutional amendment rather than making the change by judicial *fiat*, which is the way things are done these days.[23]

We need to refresh the existing checks and balances and add new ones. First, pass another amendment negating the Sixteenth amendment. As for the Federal Reserve Act, it will be subjected to the Sunset amendment described above, if enacted. This is a good start, but not nearly enough. The imbalance of power between the individual being taxes and the Federal government is so great that it is simply impossible for citizens to hold the government accountable.[24]

(7) Repeal of 16th Amendment and Amendment to Funnel *All* Tax Revenue through Protectorates

I therefore propose that taxes are collected by the protectorates which then send the money to the states, and only from the states will the Federal government receive its money. The states themselves are likewise forbidden from directly collecting taxes, relying on the protectorates to send them the collected taxes for the state's own functioning. At no time may the states or the Federal government force the remittance of the taxes by any police powers, whatsoever.

---

[23] Prohibition, and its revoking, is another example of such courtesy. Those days are gone.

[24] Every now and then, a very tiny miracle occurs, such as the case with Michael Bowman.

I am hesitant to suggest more than this. For example, should there be a 'progressive' tax? Should it be an income tax, or some other kind? Should the Federal government determine what the individual state's tax burden shall be, and then the states have the discretion to raise that amount in the manner they think is best? There are many questions and many problems with any and all ideas we might propose, but my goal here is to introduce a 'check' on the wanton spending of the various governments where few, if any, currently exist.

By funneling all the money through the protectorates and the states, there is now a way for a block of citizens to stand up to the Federal government. Combined with the newly restored status of senators as representatives of the states (and perhaps also the protectorates), if the people demand a balanced budget, they may actually be able to obtain it. If they believe circumstances warrant borrowing money from future generations, they can still do that. But if something the government is doing is so egregious as to enrage the people, the citizens within the offended protectorate can refuse to send the collected money on to the state. No individual could afford to take such a risk, but a hundred thousand individuals have enough clout to make their point.

If the protectorates within a state are all adamant together, then the state itself as a whole may refuse to send revenues to the Federal government. Therefore, there are several ways in which the Federal government is being forced to play nice with the money collected and spent by the people.

Probably, there will always be a handful of protectorates out there that stubbornly refuse to remit taxes, and there may always be one or two states that likewise put their foot down. This must be patiently endured by the Federal government, and instead of being seen as rebellious insubordination should be seen as a healthy data point for understanding just how far away from the will of the people they really are. For, if it is the case that dozens of protectorates and a third of the states are refusing to send along the tax proceeds, what it surely means is that the entity in the wrong is the Federal government. They've gone too far. They've spent money on things the people don't approve of or enacted programs they really dont want. For every protectorate or state refusing to send along funds, there are probably three or four others which want to withhold the funds, but haven't yet pulled the trigger, politically.

Note that I am not saying that the taxes won't be levied. No, I am still allowing that the taxes are collected, but they are effectively held in 'escrow' by the protectorates, and then again in 'escrow' by the states. When the states meet the terms of the 'contract' with the protectorates they are supposed to be serving, the protectorates will release their money to the states. When the Federal government meets the terms of the 'contract' with the states, the states will release their money to the Federal government.

If the states and Federal government can't enact programs which can satisfy the majority of their constituents enough that their constituents are willing to pay for the programs, it stands to reason that those programs shouldn't have been passed in the first place. Duh. If the states and Federal government have expenses which cannot survive the withholding of funds by a relatively small fraction of their constituents, they are spending too much.

A great deal of 'government' consists simply in the spending of other people's money. No matter how idealistic someone is, or how devoted to the 'common good' they are, they will not infringe on the rights and liberties of anyone unless they are being paid. No individual can stand up to the power and reach of any state or the Federal government, but hopefully my proposed mechanism will give enough clout to the citizens that they have a way of putting a dent in bureaucratic budgets, if sufficiently motivated.

It may very well be that even this isn't enough to do the job, but I stand ready to further facilitate discussion on the topic.

The next proposal relates to the exercise of police powers, itself. It is the coercive power of the state, and the monopoly it is granted to exercise it, which sets it apart from the abusive behavior of Big Business, bad journalism, and so on. As the state apparatus has expanded into every nook and cranny of human existence, so too, has the corrosive introduction of fear as the ultimate motivator for compliance. We have a word for this. It is 'totalitarianism.'

To counteract this, it is necessary to do two things. The first was the subject of the lengthy essay above, and that was to radically limit the size and scope of the state apparatus and put the fear of violence on the other foot, as it were, by putting elected officials on notice that there is a legitimate way that the people can remove them by force. The second is to further constrain how the state is able to exercise its monopoly power and what citizens can do when the state transgresses its limits. It is to this aspect I now turn.

Before we proceed it is imperative that we return to a previous point, which is that the basis of the United States, as opposed to the various European states, rests on the principles stated in the Declaration of Independence. In a nutshell: the rights of the people come from God, not the State, and thus any powers exercised by the State are delegated by the people. Anything delegated can be revoked. The 'social contract' crowd of statists have tended to be the ones who gravitate towards government (the other crowd is too busy earning a living, finding purpose and meaning in having a family, and generally minding its own business) and, with their fundamentally European outlook, have never allowed any of their power to be revoked without a bitter fight.

It is these same that often end up in Law Enforcement. This creates a tension between the "all power is delegated" crowd and the European-style "the State gives you your rights, and what the State giveth, it can taketh away" crowd which infests our bureaucracies, including police departments, sheriff's offices, and so on. The tension is simply this: the first crowd values law and order and understands very much that the job of police officers is extremely difficult and demanding, and may very well call upon the very life of the officer while he is doing his duty, and yet some police officers (and certainly the politicians and bureaucrats that manage them) don't share the fundamental values of the first crowd.

To explain this difference in outlook let me do so by a hypothetical encounter.

A police officer who believes that he is exercising power delegated to him by the citizens, who themselves receive their rights from God, upon encountering an apparently errant citizen, will take very seriously that citizen's constitutional rights. Indeed, they will be of paramount importance, almost more important than the police officer's life itself, because this police officer understands that it is this posture which preserves freedom and liberty, and prevents the people from becoming the chattel of tyrants, and, inevitably the loss of many, many more lives. The person's right to refrain from incriminating himself, the protection of his possession and papers from confiscation without due process, and simply the acknowledgement that one of the citizens delegating authority to him is the citizen right before him, will infuse the entire encounter. For such a police officer, preserving the citizen's constitutional rights throughout the event is not just an afterthought, but a prime consideration.

Alternatively, a police officer who believes that the citizens do not have any intrinsic rights, but only those which come from the State, which the officer is an agent of, will inevitably regard any non-compliance by the citizen as abject insubordination. The citizen should happily submit to the authorities, since, after all, the citizen belongs to them. If they refuse to happily submit, they should be viewed as selfish and intransigent, and treated as such. But even more inevitably than this, the police officer will adopt an attitude which aims to preserve his own life first and foremost. All that business about citizens belonging to the state will flee the mind altogether as the officer seeks to insulate himself from mortal danger. This will become the true default position of such an officer. Thus, if the citizen even flinches, such an officer, being on a hair-trigger already, will not hesitate to pull the trigger.[25]

Unless the police officer deliberately reminds himself of his first principles, even in the first case, the police officer will dispense with notions about 'rights coming from God' and pull the trigger more quickly than perhaps he ought.

Contrary to views of certain segments of the population, worries about such actions by police officers are shared by people across the political spectrum, including 'conservatives' and certainly 'libertarians.' Indeed, I would submit that 'conservatives' and 'libertarians' care about it far more than the self-proclaimed champions warring

---

[25] See the case of Daniel Shaver as a perfect example. Watch the videos.

against police brutality, as the reason why people are 'conservatives' and 'libertarians' in the first place is that they are concerned about the government having too much power. Proponents of a limited government tend to believe that people are not inherently good, which means that if given access to the levers of power, people will almost certainly, in time, abuse them. On the other hand, these proponents are under no delusion about everyone else, either, which is why they despise the 'mob.' None of us are inherently good, not even the citizens, which means that it is certain, given enough time, that citizens will behave with extreme malevolence on our streets.

Now listen carefully.

From the perspective of the Declaration of Independence and the US Constitution, citizens are fully within their rights to deal directly with *malevolent* actors, without involving the State, at all.

However, the citizens of the republic, founded on the principles of the Declaration of Independence, have delegated their authority to deal with such people to trained agents. There are many obvious advantages of this in their minds. The citizens of the republic know very well just how dangerous the job is which is precisely why they delegate it! It is precisely why they honor our soldiers and police officers (and other first responders) so much.

I suspect that whatever happens which brings us to *after*, the reclaiming of this authority by the citizens will play a large role. However, my task now is to try to save the republic, so we need to find a way to de-escalate and soften the divide between the government and the citizens. The progressive answer to such things is always to create bigger bureaucracies and centralize power even more. (They always assume that the power so centralized will always be in their hands and their hands are always as pure as the wind-driven snow!) The *real* answer is to decrease the distance between the government, with its delegated authority to use force within the law and the Constitution, and the citizens, to decentralize power.

(8) Police Powers: Amendment to Establish the Sheriff as Chief Law Enforcement Officer

I therefore propose that the role of sheriffs be codified within the Constitution itself so that it is understood absolutely that a sheriff is not concerned only with law and order within his jurisdiction, but is also the chief protector of the rights and liberties of the citizens. This duty would include demanding that other law enforcement agencies, such as at the state and federal level, operate within the parameters of the Constitution when they act within the sheriff's jurisdiction. This duty would include openly defying the other agencies, up to and including coming to the aid of citizens whose rights are being thrown into jeopardy... up to and including using force to do so.

I can already see people wringing their hands about this proposal. Right now, sheriffs tend to work hand in glove with the other law enforcement agencies, and this spirit of cooperation has many important benefits. However, unless we want to make it easier for citizens to shoot at officers when they feel they are being engaged unlawfully by the authorities, we need to take seriously this idea that such authorities are delegated, and ensure that there is at least one law enforcement agency which is poised to have an adversarial relationship with other law enforcement agencies.

When people go to court, they are entitled to representation. The adversarial nature of our court system has proven, in the main, to be an effective way to ensure that the accused citizen—being in relation to the state disproportionately powerless—is able to defend himself. I am proposing we extend that adversarial system to the agents in the field, as it were, exercising the delegated powers of the people to use violence if necessary.

On this proposal, an average citizen has the same rights and privileges of opposing unlawful actions by law enforcement that they do now. The only difference is that he now has an ally who is legally authorized to stand by his side.

The sheriff becomes the chief law enforcement agent within the jurisdiction, outranking all others. The police chiefs of cities answer to them, and the state police and federal agents operate within the jurisdiction only at the pleasure and permission of the sheriff. If these other law enforcement agencies cannot persuade the sheriff that they have a proper basis for acting within the jurisdiction, the sheriff has the authority to utterly prevent them from doing so. If these other agencies abuse the privileges to operate within the jurisdiction when granted, the sheriff may remove those privileges.

At present, sheriffs are organized along the lines of counties. So, you will have one sheriff for each county. This has its advantages and its problems. Without getting into them, **let me propose this as the solution: for every 100,000 people there will be at least one sheriff who is elected by the same.** Regions which are not so densely populated may still be served by a county sheriff. More densely populated areas, such as large metropolitan areas, will have to create new sheriff positions. The lines demarcating their jurisdictions can be revised every ten years, just as is the case with redistricting.

Sheriffs are always elected and all other law enforcement agents within the jurisdiction are ultimately subordinate to the sheriff.

By this mechanism, we bring the most powerful law enforcement agent any citizen has to answer to much closer to the citizens themselves. It becomes much more practical for a sheriff to know the citizens and be known by them. It becomes much more practical for a sheriff to execute the laws in a manner the citizens expect and demand.

By this mechanism, we create a hard divide between the politicians and the ones executing the law. The politicians may make all the laws that they want, but if the sheriff, with the support of the citizens within his jurisdiction, deem those laws unconstitutional, then there is no police power those politicians can dispatch within the jurisdiction which do not have to answer to the sheriff—who is authorized to use force against other agencies, just as if they were the citizens themselves resisting the chains of tyrants.

Naturally, sheriffs themselves may become corrupt. They are subject to the same removal amendments I have already proposed. It may be necessary to provide a provision by which neighboring sheriffs, or perhaps the protectorate, can remove a sheriff when corruption exists or the sheriff himself uses or authorizes force which is outside the parameters of the Constitution and the will of the sheriff's own citizens.

My proposal would radically alter the landscape as far as law enforcement goes, but I think a somewhat uneasy equilibrium will be met, in which the following statement becomes the *status quo*:

"When government fears the people, there is liberty. When the people fear the government, there is tyranny."[26]

(9) Amendment to Restrict Emergency Powers

Finally, recent events have made it clear that even if something is explicitly enumerated in the Bill of Rights, this will not stop authorities from trampling on it. All they need is the right pre-text.

Historically speaking, the Bill of Rights was, strictly speaking, a restraint on the Federal

---

[26] Commonly attributed to Thomas Jefferson, but probably first said by John Basil Barnhill in 1914. True, no matter who said it, or when.

government. This is probably not what the founders intended. When they said things like Congress shall make no laws prohibiting "the right of the people peaceably to assemble," they did not imagine that it would then be ok for the individual states to prohibit the peaceable assembly of citizens. That is, the framers probably never imagined that a state would tell itself that the Bill of Rights was not for *them*. The early constitutions of the various states seem to suggest that most of the states did not think that way at all. Moreover, the tenth amendment, part of the original Bill of Rights, indicates that whatever restrictions apply to the Federal government do not fall exclusively to the states. Here is the text:

> The powers not delegated to the United States by the Constitution, nor prohibited by it to the States, are reserved to the States respectively, **or to the people.**

Emphasis added.

While much heat has been generated by opposing the Federal government against the States within this framework, very few people have seen fit to point out that the phrase "or to the people" is right there in the text, as well. The tenth amendment makes it clear that not even the States can trample on the rights of the people.

Now, this ended up being a big mess, as many readers know very well. The States would proceed to abuse their own people, even going so far as to refusing to acknowledge that some people were people at all. To rectify this—following a bloody conflict which killed more than a half a million people—the fourteenth amendment was passed. This amendment has proved to be a very imperfect remedy, inspiring a weird kind of judicial activism. The Supreme Court, by invoking the fourteenth amendment as if it were a magic wand, made the rights enumerated in the Bill of Rights (and a whole host of other 'rights' not in the text at all, as it turns out!) apply to the states just as those rights applied to the Federal government. This process, called 'incorporation,' selectively and slowly worked its way through the enumerated rights. Meanwhile, there was, all along, the clause "or to the people" right there in the tenth amendment to do it once and for all and be done with it.[27]

To put it another way, the tenth amendment does *not* say, "The powers not delegated to the United States by the Constitution, nor prohibited by it to the States, are reserved to the States respectively, or to the counties, or to the cities, or townships."

No.

The founders wanted to make it absolutely clear that except for the powers enumerated in the Constitution, the Federal government would do nothing else. They imagined that the States would be the place where the people crafted their own unique

---

[27] Ironies above ironies, the tenth amendment, which explicitly affirms that all of the rights not expressly granted to the Federal government belong *to the people*, has not been incorporated, even though the whole point of incorporation is to take the Bill of Rights and apply them *to the people*.

ways of governing. They didn't imagine that the States would effectively become federations of their own. Except, unlike with our Federal government, the Federalized-States do not have corresponding "Bills of Rights" which are *reserved to the people*. This omission has encouraged the States to play fast and loose with the rights of the people.

This must be fixed. I believe my proposals already laid out will go a long way to fixing it.

That said, I think we need one more thing to go into the US Constitution. **Something like this proposal:**

No invocation of emergency powers can extend beyond 45 days unless the legislature *of the jurisdiction affected* approves of it. Any extension of emergency powers beyond 90 days is only permissible if the citizens of the jurisdiction themselves approve of it in a referendum.

Under the guise of the pandemic and its 'emergency,' various governmental bodies have seen fit to do whatever they want for as long as they want by invoking emergency powers. The present mechanisms available to the people for telling those governments to shove it where the sun doesn't shine, or, alternatively, "Thank you sir, may I have another?", are wholly inadequate to the task. We have the astonishing situation where people in rural areas have requirements imposed on them as if they lived in cities, and it takes persuading a million or more people that the requirements are completely unreasonable for their own locale.

The justification for such things is often bundled up in the complaint by those who seem to delight a great deal in imposing their views on other people that "this shouldn't be about politics!" What they think they mean by this is that the matters in question are so obvious and founded on fact that any reasonable person would accede to the recommendations of 'experts' without hesitation, 'for their own good,' and of course, 'for the common good.'

But what they *actually* mean is that the people should not be allowed to determine for themselves how they shall be governed, for that is what it means to say something is 'political.' To say something is 'political' means it is something that is subjected to the political processes, by which we settle our differences through the ballot box rather than by bullets. To argue that all of these restrictions are not 'political' is to say, in actual fact, that they will *not* be subject to the ballot box. Which means, eventually, addressing the restrictions with bullets.

That seems less than ideal to me.

As I have been arguing throughout, the key to bringing back a civil society where freedom and liberty is real and preserved is to remove as many things as possible from the realm of 'politics', leaving only the most essential matters to government. 'Essential' is defined as those issues which are really undeniable, that the people, as a whole, see fit to delegate to the government.

The problem with the view that so many things are

"so obvious and founded on fact" (as established by *our* experts and *our* scientists!) is that in reality, anything really so obvious and truly founded on facts will be, by its very definition, uncontroversial. It is only when things are not obvious, when the facts do not speak self-evidently, when the application of moral principles are not simple, that we have controversy at all, and consequently, a need to utilize the political process.

In other words, if something really is self-evident, no law is required. The imposition of the law or the use of the government is a tacit admission that the thing in question is not self-evident. It is probably not something that is 'purely scientific.' There almost certainly is ambiguity. The more controversy, the more it is shrieked that "this shouldn't be about politics!", the more 'political' it is to those who make that claim, and the more imperative to engage the political processes. ASAP.

Allow me to illustrate.

At one side of the spectrum where no law is necessary because something is really self-evident, we have the matter of eating. There are no laws requiring people to eat because people do not need to be told to eat. Granted, the progressive crowd very much would like to tell people what they should eat and relish the prospects of bringing the coercive powers of the state to bear on the question, but even so, even they don't think you need a law to tell people to eat.

Then, in cases where people have been willing to pass laws without there being much associated heat, there is a class of laws where the thing desired is, truly, not controversial. This class of laws are the ones that basically establish the framework for interacting safely and efficiently. For example, traffic laws. What is "obvious and founded on fact" is that most people want to be able to drive down the road without being smashed into by another driver. Thus, there isn't a single person in the country (and this is not hyperbole) that is upset by the law requiring people to drive on the right side of the road. There isn't a single person in the country who objects to having traffic lights use the color red to indicate 'stop.' Even those in a habit of running red lights are counting on their fellow drivers remaining still while the light is red.

These types of things *really are* self-evident.

If there is controversy and differences of opinion, you can be absolutely certain that the issue at hand is not self-evident. It is not 100% established scientific 'fact.' It is not. If it was, as I said, no law would be necessary, except, perhaps, for providing that 'framework for interacting safely and efficiently', as indicated above.

Which brings me to those times when circumstances are such where there is a severe jolt to the *status quo*. We call these situations 'emergencies,' and there is a sense in which the whole purpose of the government is to be prepared for just these kinds of eventualities. The whole purpose of first responders is to respond to emergencies. We have a mayor because in the management of the city, it is inevitable that something will come up which requires a decision 'on the spot.' Sure, many of those kinds of decisions are not life and death, but they are still things you don't want to have to submit to the voters each and every time they come up.

In real emergencies, special provisions are in place for the duration, but then disappear once the emergency is over. For example, traffic may be stopped while first responders extricate an injured driver. When the driver is rescued and the debris cleared and the accident investigation completed, things go back to normal.

Real emergencies are short in duration.

Emergency powers exist for a reason. They were created 'by the people' and delegated to certain individuals to act quickly when decisive action is required due to unexpected and sometimes difficult circumstances. Unfortunately, as is often the case, the people didn't imagine that even these powers could be abused indefinitely and at the sole discretion of the authorities. Sufficient checks and balances were not included. I believe this needs to be addressed at the highest levels. That is, in our most important document.

The people must be consulted perpetually in order for self-government to be a real thing. An 'emergency' is not something that lasts for a year or longer. If something lasts that long, it isn't a 'traffic accident,' it's a thing to be managed by the people themselves. At the very least, it falls into the class of laws in which we hash out how we are going to 'interact safely and efficiently,' which, despite being matters where necessity spurs less controversy (theoretically), is nonetheless determined via the political process.

Apparently, our system is so top-heavy and corrupt that we need to spell this out. What a shame.

With the addition of this amendment, and the amendments already listed, I believe we can handle most other abuses that are related to the handling of the pandemic, so I will say no more about *that*.

(10?) On the Abuses by Businesses

There is one remaining matter which needs to be addressed head-on but for which I do not at present have an answer that I find satisfactory. This is the abuse by Big Business, Big Tech, and Big Media.

I am willing to delegate to the governments the right to keep monopolies from occurring, because monopolies do not merely enrich single individuals or corporations at the expense of other individuals and corporations. They tend, also, to corrupt and corrode the public order and can even compromise national security.

In other words, there is a wider public interest than mere economics when we think about ensuring businesses are in competition against each other. The argument is often made that forcing businesses to compete against each other ensures that consumers have the best possible products and services, as the businesses strive to out-do and out-perform each other. This is certainly true, but then, I'm not sure if that in itself warrants bringing to bear the coercive powers of the state. The other thing accomplished by forcing businesses to compete against each other is that this serves as a 'check and balance' within these operations.

Businesses can act corruptly and abuse their station just as any other entity can. The way that we handle such abuses in other realms (if you are a constitutionalist) is to introduce checks and balances. The more the potential for abuse, the more checks and balances we introduce. This is the whole purpose of this present document, if you haven't noticed. A business which has to compete against other businesses will by necessity restrain itself when its pursuit of profit stands a good chance of backfiring dramatically, allowing a competitor to gain market share.

However, there are commercial operations which are very large, but not necessarily monopolies, which are poisoning our society in a number of important ways. For one thing, they have decided, on their own, to not merely be commercial in nature, but to *be political*. That is, they wish to act within the political arena, as for-profit corporations.

Our system already has provisions for organizations acting within the political arena. They can register as such and are regarded as such. There is transparency. These commercial operations effectively are acting on 'false pretenses.'

On top of that, they have the ability to muzzle or even silence those who have different viewpoints. This is especially problematic, as some of them have been given special protections to immunize themselves from the consequences of the viewpoints expressed through their products, and yet they still see fit to censor viewpoints. This, as they sold themselves initially as 'neutral' platforms where various viewpoints would be expressed, and becoming a primary place where those viewpoints would be expressed, thus requiring the protections.

In an infamous example, Facebook argued that its users did not have a right to privacy since anyone who uses their platform essentially is like someone walking through a public square, where there is no expectation of privacy. However, on a public square, it is not permissible to prohibit free speech—which is something that Facebook thinks it should be able to do. So, in their view, they are like a public square when it benefits them financially, but they are not a public square when it harms them politically.

This kind of arrangement cannot be allowed to persist.

The problem is that I don't know how to fix it, because I trust the current governing authorities as much as I trust the businesses in question. Which is to say, I don't trust them at all. Further involving the government in matters of commerce is something that makes me very uncomfortable and which I do not desire. But when the businesses themselves *become governments in their own right,* something must be done to introduce sufficient checks and balances to preserve freedom, liberty, and self-government.

I leave it to further conversations to come up with a

remedy for this powder-keg problem.

Conclusion

Aleksandr Solzhenitsyn said, in a speech reprinted in the 1976 book *Warning to the West*:

> "Don't call a wolf to help you against the dogs." If dogs are attacking and tearing at you, fight against the dogs; do not call a wolf for help. Because when the wolves come, they will destroy the dogs or drive them away, but they will tear you apart as well.

Solzhenitsyn was rebuking the West for allying with the Soviets during World War 2 and allowing totalitarianism to rise in China, but I find that the Russian proverb he cites can be applied in another way, as well, which I don't think he'd disagree with. It is tempting for 'conservatives' to try to resolve the problems created by Big Government with even more Big Government. This is unquestionably what the 'left' does, the only difference being that the 'conservatives' understand how the problems were created in the first place, while the 'left' remains completely oblivious. There is a sad irony to the fact that the people who know where the problem is nonetheless seek to resolve it through the same path that brought them headaches in the first place.

I saw this attitude most vividly in the rise of the 'Tea Party' in 2010. There were certainly many people who properly understood the problem and these were elected to office throughout the country. But not quite enough of them. There remained a larger share of 'Republicans' who chastised the newly elected firebrands for being "unwilling to govern." So, attempts to scale back the size and scope of various governments were held back, not just by the Democrats, which was to be expected, but by the more 'level-headed' of the Republicans.

Of course, why 'governing' entails creating, sustaining, and expanding the government but never eliminating or reducing the reach of the government was never asked, let alone answered.

At any rate, it has been my firm belief that more recent affairs, some of which cause consternation even to the most liberty-loving libertarian-minded persons, are the fault of these more 'mature' Republicans failing to deliver on the mandates given to counties, states, and Congress over three consecutive elections. For, apart from the presidency in 2012, the Republican Party grew in size and popularity, not just in 2010, but also in 2012 and 2014. When 2016 rolled around, the Republican 'base' had contempt for *even their own* establishment figures.

They didn't choose Trump for his charisma. They chose him because the 'base' figured they had nothing left to lose, with their own party having sold them out while squandering fairly commanding majorities. Notably, Ted Cruz was the last remaining 'establishment' figure to hold out, not one of those more 'mature' individuals 'willing to govern,' like, say, Jeb Bush, who was drummed out early. Of all the establishment figures who ran in 2016, it was Cruz who was most likely to deliver on the Tea Party promise. But even he could not overcome the cynicism of most Republicans and many independents.[28]

Trump has certainly not been a proponent of a smaller government! He has, however, governed more as a Republican than almost any Republican has before him. Nonetheless, it seems unlikely that he will be able to take the problem out at the knees and put us on the path necessary to keep the republic intact. He is still operating within the parameters of a system deeply undermined by hundreds of years of decaying foundations and bloated government over-reach. The debt was increasing, notwithstanding the response to COVID.

Many people believe that the best thing that Trump has done has bought us *time*. This manifesto is written in the spirit of the idea that maybe, *just maybe*, we have enough time to stop the wobbling of the republic from finally teetering into the abyss. Maybe, just maybe, we can restore the foundations. Maybe.

It was in that spirit that I issued my proposals. Knowing full well that various adjustments to the Constitution would have to be made to get the

---

[28] The 2018 taking of the House of Representatives by the Democrats, and various Democrat governorship wins, probably still was the result of Republicans bailing on their mandates. In the case of the House, it was literally bailing… dozens and dozens retired rather be around to deal with the Trump-Russia 'collusion' madness. Why anyone, least of all 'Republicans,' believes the accusations of Democrats or the MSM is beyond me.

principles to 'fit,' and knowing full well that merely passing the amendments would not be enough to see them enforced,[29] that was still the project I set before myself.

My larger goal was to start the conversation about what we shall do *after*. We have time to have that conversation. We have time to plan and organize for that eventuality. We don't know what will bring about the end or which of us will still be standing at that time, but hopefully there will be enough of us around to point our communities in the right direction.

Probably, any such movement will have to run parallel to a spiritual revival. Such a revival would be welcome, but unfortunately, the way these things go, before people turn to God in repentance, they must first feel the crushing weight of the consequences of their own actions. Such was the case of Pharaoh and the Egyptians. Such was the case of Nebuchadnezzar. Such has been the case for myself, and I'm sure many of my readers. This means that, before our country and countrymen can be refreshed and renewed, they must first drink the cup of sorrows that lead to repentance.

Let us prepare for the drinking of this cup even as we stand ready to bring to people a hope far larger than can be secured by mortal men on this transient earth.

---

[29] The Constitution, as written, hasn't been enforced consistently as it is, so it is a long shot, to say the least, to hope that new amendments would be enforced. I dare say, I would not be surprised if SCOTUS declared an actual amendment to the Constitution to be unconstitutional, and a very large part of the population willing to abide a ruling to that effect.

Back to Solzhenitsyn.

I anticipate that some will say that my proposals are still fairly complicated and look an awful lot like 'Big Government.' Well, I was trying to remain compatible with our existing system, so there is that. But I answer the charge by saying that my proposed measures, complicated though they might be, divide and redistribute power and place the levers of the most impactful powers much closer to the hands of the people. This was the original intent of the Constitution. I have merely determined that the Constitution did not go far enough and so sought to secure that intent more vigorously.

We must resist the instinct to unite and centralize power, and place the levers of power even further in the hands of politicians who live far from us, and bureaucrats who are even further away. For as much comfort as we might take knowing that 'our' people are at those levers, history leaves no doubt that other people may take hold of those levers. One only needs to look back a couple of years, or less, to see the truth of that. Whatever we can do to decentralize power now, we should do. My belief is that *after*, if we're lucky, decentralized power will be the *de facto* situation. If we aren't so lucky, we'll be living in a totalitarian state, and these considerations will remain theoretical, if not treasonous.

Therein, I think, is part of the current problem. Even 'Republicans' will oppose my proposals. How much more our 'progressive' neighbors, who cannot sleep peacefully at night knowing that two thousand miles away, someone is having a good time. The problem with CHAZ is not CHAZ, but with the fact that they would have CHAZ erected at the national and even global level. No such 'autonomous zones' have ever been satisfied remaining a mere *zone*. Any proposal, let alone the ones I've proposed which double-down on 'small government' principles, will prompt the most violent outrage. You don't even have to try to implement them. Their mere expression could get you bashed in the face. Or worse.

And yet, I still believe it is more or less the way forward. We 'conservatives' are going to have to learn to live with the fact that many people elsewhere in our own country don't want to live according to the values and principles which we know bring freedom to mind, body, and soul. When we say 'small government,' we're going to have to really mean it. Unless it really is for the 'common good,' unless it really is for protecting human life, unless it really is indisputably preserving human rights, whether it be locally or Federal, we're just going to have to keep it out of the hands of the government. Even if *we're* in charge of it… today.

I therefore propose that like-minded individuals begin a conversation with me about how to bring these principles to bear in our current situation. I will consider it an honor and a privilege to facilitate these conversations. Maybe we will be able to translate those conversations into concrete action. The United States is worth the shot, in my opinion.

But, more likely, our efforts will be more fruitful

after. Thus, I further propose that we all meet together, in a time and place to be chosen from out of the rubble, at a new Constitutional Convention. Those of us who survive, that is.

Sell your cloak and buy one.

To Join the Conversation

Visit

www.constitutionalistmanifesto.com

Then all the elders of Israel gathered themselves together and came to Samuel to Ramah. They said to him, "Behold, you are old, and your sons don't walk in your ways. Now make us a king to judge us like all the nations." But the thing displeased Samuel when they said, "Give us a king to judge us."

Samuel prayed to Yahweh. Yahweh said to Samuel, "Listen to the voice of the people in all that they tell you; for they have not rejected you, but they have rejected me as the king over them. According to all the works which they have done since the day that I brought them up out of Egypt even to this day, in that they have forsaken me and served other gods, so they also do to you. Now therefore, listen to their voice. However, you shall protest solemnly to them, and shall show them the way of the king who will reign over them."

Samuel told all Yahweh's words to the people who asked him for a king. He said, "This will be the way of the king who shall reign over you: he will take your sons and appoint them as his servants, for his chariots and to be his horsemen; and they will run before his chariots. He will appoint them to him for captains of thousands and captains of fifties; and he will assign some to plow his ground and to reap his harvest; and to make his instruments of war and the instruments of his chariots. He will take your daughters to be perfumers, to be cooks, and to be bakers. He will take your fields, your vineyards, and your olive groves, even your best, and give them to his servants. He will take one tenth of your seed and of your vineyards, and give it to his officers and to his servants. He will take your male servants, your female servants, your best young men, and your donkeys, and assign them to his own work. He will take one tenth of your flocks; and you will be his servants. You will cry out in that day because of your king whom you will have chosen for yourselves; and Yahweh will not answer you in that day."

1 Samuel 8

www.ingramcontent.com/pod-product-compliance
Lightning Source LLC
Chambersburg PA
CBHW010236100426
42813CB00011B/2630